THE WOMEN
WHO SPIED
FOR BRITAIN

THE WOMEN WHO SPIED FOR BRITAIN

ROBYN WALKER

AMBERLEY

Cover illustrations: Front cover: Violette Szabo (Susan Ottaway); Violette Szabo's ID card (David Harrison); A female parachutist (J. & C. McCutcheon Collection). *Back cover:* Mass parachute descent (J. & C. McCutcheon Collection).

First published in 2015

Amberley Publishing
The Hill, Stroud
Gloucestershire, GL5 4EP

www.amberley-books.com

ISBN 978 1 4456 4584 1 (paperback)
ISBN 978 1 4456 2316 0 (ebook)

British Library Cataloguing in Publication Data.
A catalogue record for this book is available from the British Library.

Typesetting and Origination by Amberley Publishing
Printed in the UK.

Contents

Foreword by HRH The Princess Royal

As Commandant-in-Chief of the First Aid Nursing Yeomanry and Patron of the Special Forces Club, I am delighted to write a foreword for this book highlighting the valuable contributions made by women during the Second World War, whose courage in the face of danger was extraordinary. Britain's Special Operations Executive (SOE) recruited many women throughout the war, not only to serve as secret agents but also to work as coders, signallers, agent conductors and administrative staff at the agent training facilities. Most of these women were commissioned into the FANY Corps.

This well-researched history of the women who helped to ensure victory for Britain draws on primary-source material, interviews with both family members and colleagues of the agents, and the most current available research, to present a comprehensive picture of the women the Special Operations Executive employed. It provides a fascinating account of their motivation for service and, in some cases, of their tragic ends in service of the country. None of these brave women aspired to be heroes but without them the Resistance movements in France, and across the continent, would not have been as successful as they were, and we owe them all a huge debt of gratitude.

Anne

Acknowledgements

This book is the result of dogged determination on the part of the author, the foresight of a commissioning editor who thought it stood a chance and the kindness and generosity of people across the world who were willing to share.

Throughout this manuscript's journey to publication I was continuously amazed by the wonderful responses I received from perfect strangers, who always seemed to have time to help me with my research. Robert Maloubier was the first and his offer to share his knowledge of SOE and the details of Violette Szabo's final mission was truly a gift. The assistance of Martyn Cox has been immeasurable. His willingness to provide contacts, and to share information and photographs, is much appreciated. Thanks also to David Harrison, a gentleman who is so clearly passionate about the subject of SOE agents, for his help in obtaining photographs.

I was privileged to be able to speak with Nadya Murdoch (daughter of Sonia Butt d'Artois) and appreciate so much her taking the time to chat with me about her mother and to provide me with some lovely photos.

Many, many thanks to author Susan Ottaway, whose work I have long admired. That such an esteemed author would take the time to correspond with me and share her resources means so much and I am truly grateful.

Much appreciation goes out to all of the individuals who provided photographs and photograph permissions for this book. Your willingness to share has truly enhanced the project. Special mention to John Horrocks and the Tilford Bach Society, who went above and beyond to get me a photo I desperately wanted, and to the Special Forces Club for their support.

My thanks are also extended to HRH Princess Anne for agreeing to write the Foreword for this book. Her willingness to be a part of this journey was most gracious and her contribution was most welcome.

I offer my sincere gratitude to my editor, Emily Brewer at Amberley Publishing, for not only her belief in the project but for her constant support and assistance. She calmed my panic when things seemed overwhelming, she provided excellent contacts and research advice and she was, quite simply, an amazing advocate for this book. I owe her an incredible debt of gratitude. Also, many years ago an editor named Casey Cornelius gave me hope that this manuscript could actually become a book and her feedback on the writing was quite valuable. Thank you.

Finally, I would like to thank my husband Terry and son Jed for their love and support throughout this journey, especially when things seemed bleak; Corrina Austin, whose friendship and writing talents continue to inspire me; Ron Biekx for his feedback and willingness to proofread; and the rest of my family, who encouraged my interest in the Second World War and who are always willing to buy my books.

Introduction

Women were an active and integral part of the Allied war effort during the Second World War. They worked a variety of positions including driving ambulances and ferrying planes, nursing, decoding intelligence messages, operating barrage balloons, serving as air-raid wardens, manning anti-aircraft guns and radar stations, providing ground communications with Allied pilots and filling factory positions left vacant by men who had enlisted. Yet these were purely non-combatant situations. Never would these women be in a position to come face to face with the enemy, since military policy, in the British, Canadian and American armed forces, made no allowances for female combatants. However, a select group of women actually did find their way to the front lines – and, indeed, beyond them. These women trained with men, served with men and, in some cases, even commanded men. They assumed possibly the most dangerous position of the war – the role of secret agent.

In response to the German invasion of Poland, France and Britain declared war on Germany on 3 September 1939. During the spring of 1940 the Germans launched a full-scale attack on Western Europe, taking first Norway and Denmark (April) then proceeding to smash through the defences of the Netherlands, Belgium and France (May). The British Expeditionary Force (BEF), which was stationed in France, was forced back to the beaches of Dunkirk, on the French coast. While the majority of the BEF was evacuated off the beaches of Dunkirk, almost all of their heavy equipment and vehicles were left behind. By the end of the summer of 1940 the Germans controlled all of Western Europe, and Great Britain and Canada stood virtually alone (the United States did not enter the war until December 1941) against the Germans. With most of their military machinery lost at Dunkirk, Great Britain began a massive rebuilding campaign to rearm and resupply their shattered army. They also began focusing their attentions on less traditional forms of warfare.

The Special Operations Executive (SOE) was established by Britain in July 1940 and its mission was to undertake sabotage, subversion and intelligence gathering against the German enemy as well as assisting resistance groups in the occupied countries. Churchill ordered SOE to 'set Europe ablaze' with a wide variety of subversive actions. SOE's headquarters was located on Baker Street, in London. It was organised into country sections, with each section being responsible for conducting covert operations within their designated country. The branch of SOE responsible for operations in France was known as 'F' Section. 'F' Section's purpose was to establish networks or circuits of subversive agents throughout France. These networks, almost always named after a certain profession (i.e. CLERGYMAN, SALESMAN, WRESTLER), operated independently of one another but their geographic territories often overlapped. The networks also worked closely with the French Resistance, which consisted of French civilians who were determined to fight against the German military occupation of France. Armed bands of Resistance members were known as the Maquis.

SOE agents were sent into occupied territories to perform a number of different functions. Intelligence gathering was vital. Information that was gathered about the strength, positions and movements of German forces, and the location and output of German military factories, was invaluable to the Allied commanders when it came time to plan military ground attacks or bombing raids. Agents were also involved in leading sabotage missions against German communications (e.g. cutting telephone lines), transportation (e.g. destroying sections of rail line) and industry (e.g. blowing up factories), and in training local Resistance fighters in the use of arms and explosives. Agents sent in to work as couriers were expected to travel freely throughout cities and the countryside, transporting messages (often mission instructions) from agents throughout the region and carrying intelligence reports back to the network's wireless operator. This was often hazardous work, as the courier could not remain hidden but had to be out in public where they could be subject to a random search or arrest. By meeting with other agents and carrying messages, the courier was always at risk. The job of the wireless operator was to transmit all of the network's messages back to London. This too was hazardous work, since German radio detection devices were extremely effective at tracking transmission sites. The wireless operator had to stay mobile in order to keep ahead of the German detection equipment, and it was difficult to travel with the bulky wireless sets. Moreover, if the wireless operator was caught with his or her radio it was a dead giveaway that the individual was working as a secret agent. All agents employed by SOE, no matter what assignment they were trained for, had to be adaptable. An agent who was sent in as a wireless operator could just as easily find him or herself doing courier work as assisting in blowing up a convoy.

Working as a secret agent was fraught with peril. From the moment they left Great Britain, agents faced countless dangerous situations. Parachuting always carried with it an element of danger, and many agents, including Christine Granville and Sonia Butt, were injured upon landing. Sometimes there would be a reception committee (usually members of the Resistance) waiting for the agent, to guide them through unfamiliar territory and help them link up with their network. Sometimes, there was no one to greet the agent, and they were forced to make their way on their own. Occasionally, the Germans would be waiting, as in the case of poor Madeleine Damerment, and this meant certain arrest and incarceration, and quite possibly execution. If an agent managed to land safely and link up with their network, a variety of other dangers lurked around every corner. It was imperative that an agent be able to maintain their cover, and if their fake identification cards failed to pass scrutiny, their French accent was not perfect or they were caught with something as simple as an English matchbook in their pocket, their cover could be blown and they would find themselves quickly taken into German custody. Even if an agent maintained an impeccable cover, there was always the threat that someone, be it a French civilian who was looking for a reward (such as Renée Garry) or a captured fellow agent (such as Mathilde Carré) who was looking to save their own life, might betray them. Yet perhaps the biggest threat to all undercover agents was the fact that they were operating outside the protection of the Geneva Convention. Amendments made to the Geneva Convention in 1925 basically set out rules for the treatment of prisoners of war. Lawful combatants (those who were part of the regular armed forces and who engaged in combat *openly*) were afforded certain protections upon capture. Undercover agents, however, were considered unlawful combatants (because of the covert nature of their work) and thus were afforded no protection. Once captured, an undercover agent could expect horrific treatment, often culminating in torture and death. All SOE agents were warned of this possibility when they were recruited.

Although military policy clearly restricted women to non-combatant roles, SOE actively recruited them. This was done for a variety of reasons. Firstly, SOE recognised early on that women could make effective undercover agents. The work of women such as Nancy Wake and Christine Granville, who had both been working with Resistance movements before coming to Britain, was well known to SOE. Secondly, language qualifications were probably the most important thing SOE recruiters were looking for, since it was imperative that undercover agents be able to blend in with their surroundings. By expanding their pool of multilingual recruits to include both males and females, SOE was able to increase its number of agents substantially. Thirdly, most of the young men in German-occupied countries were expected to work in the war industry. Young men wandering the cities or countryside, seemingly unemployed, would arouse German suspicion. SOE recognised that women would have much more freedom of movement, which would be key to promoting SOE's subversive agenda in Occupied Europe.

Of the women who worked either formally or informally as secret agents during the Second World War, most were employed by SOE's 'F' Section. Some worked with local Resistance groups based in their own countries, while others were employed by the American Office of Strategic Services (OSS). Despite their differences in organisation, age, and ethnic and socio-economic backgrounds, all of the women shared a keen sense of adventure and a willingness to put their lives on the line for a cause which they believed in. Some survived the war unscathed; others had their bodies and spirits broken during captivity and torture, while a number simply did not survive. All of them have unique stories that deserve to be told.

Violette Szabo (1921–45)
Code Name: Louise

Devastatingly beautiful and endowed with a sparkling personality, Violette Szabo captivated everyone who made her acquaintance. Her story could almost be a work of fiction. A lovely young mother, widowed after the Germans killed her husband, seeks revenge upon the enemy by enlisting as an undercover agent. Yet Szabo did not enjoy the happy ending that an author could have penned for her. Her ending came tragically, at the hands of those whom she hated most.

Violette Szabo was born Violette Reine Elizabeth Bushell, in the town of Levallois-Perret, France, on 26 June 1921. With her French mother and English father, Violette spent the first few years of her life living in France, before her family, which included an older brother, Roy, moved to Britain. Violette's family struggled financially and life was not easy. Although Violette's father did find steady work as a bus driver and her mother made dresses, the family found it difficult to support their two children, and sometime around 1926/7 Violette and Roy were sent back to France to live with relatives. Over the next couple of years, Violette saw very little of her parents, but enjoyed her time in France and became a fluent French speaker. Around the age of eleven,

Violette returned to Britain to live with her family, which now included brothers John and Noel. Another brother, Richard, would follow in 1935. The Bushells lived in South London and, by all accounts, Violette was a popular young girl who was athletic and adventurous. Photographs show that she was stunningly beautiful. School proved a challenge at first, since Violette had been raised speaking French rather than English, but she worked hard at her courses and was soon completely bilingual. Her mates nicknamed her 'Froggy' as she still spoke French quite often, especially at home. In 1935 the Bushell family moved to a home at 18 Burnley Road, and a plaque dedicated to Violette is mounted there today, reading

VIOLETTE
SZABO, G.C.
1921–1945
Secret Agent
lived here
SHE GAVE HER LIFE
FOR THE FRENCH
RESISTANCE

It was while living at Burnley Road that Violette demonstrated exactly how determined and adventurous she was. She left school at fourteen and worked as a sales assistant at a department store. It was a job she hated, but each day she faithfully showed up to sweep and dust, and fetch tea for the other staff. One night, however, she had a vicious argument with her father. Fed up with her father and her job, fourteen-year-old Violette packed a bag, grabbed her passport and boarded a boat to France. After an uneventful Channel crossing, she arrived on French soil and fearlessly made her way from the port to her aunt's house, only to discover that her aunt was not home. Other fourteen-year-olds might have panicked in this situation but Violette remained calm. She eventually tracked down her aunt, who was stunned to discover that her young niece had arrived all alone, and word was sent to Violette's parents that she was safe. After a few days' holiday in France, which gave Violette a chance to recover her good temper, her aunt helped her board a return boat to Britain, ending her rather incredible runaway adventure. Unfortunately her 'spirit of adventure' was not appreciated by her employer, and upon her return Violette discovered that her absence from work had resulted in her employment being terminated.

Violette spent the next several years working a variety of jobs, including working as a shop girl at Woolworth's and at the perfume counter at the Bon Marché department store. She enjoyed cycling and shooting with her friends and dated several young men. One, Sydney Matthews, remembered that Violette was 'a very pretty girl and great fun to be with'.[1] Although war clouds were spreading over Europe, Violette showed little interest in the impending conflict. Parties, sporting activities and casual dating filled Violette's days. Nobody could have predicted that this pretty young shop girl would be the first female ever awarded the George Cross, Britain's highest civilian award for acts of heroism and courage in the face of grave danger.

In September 1939, Germany invaded Poland. Great Britain and France declared war on Germany, but for several months, although arms production and mobilisation of troops accelerated (for example, the British Expeditionary Force, BEF, was sent to France to reinforce the Franco-Belgian border), little took place in terms of armed conflict. Then, suddenly, on 10 May 1940, German armies flooded into the Netherlands and Belgium. By 14 May the Germans had entered France, smashing through the Ardennes Forest and sending the French and British troops reeling back towards the English Channel. There, they were pinned down on the beaches, desperately trying to maintain a defensive perimeter and hoping, at least on the part of the British, to be evacuated back to Britain.

By summer, Britain was a virtual hotbed of activity; France had fallen to the Germans. The BEF, and many French and Belgian soldiers, had been successfully evacuated from the French beaches but all of the military equipment had been left behind. Fears were running high about the possibility of a German invasion. Violette's father became an air-raid warden and her brother Roy joined the Army. Soldiers newly arrived from the British Commonwealth (Canada, New Zealand and Australia), as well as foreign soldiers who had escaped from Occupied Europe, filled English cities and towns. Violette decided to do her part, and joined the Land Army where she was assigned the job of picking strawberries. Although the job itself was quite enjoyable, Violette was certain that she was capable of more important things, and she returned home after the picking season to plan her next move. However, before Violette was able to determine her plan of action, fate intervened. On 14 July, Bastille Day, Violette's mother sent her out to see if she could find a French soldier who might appreciate a home-cooked meal and some French conversation. Violette and a friend went into London to the parade that was being sponsored by the Free French Forces (the Resistance organisation founded by Charles de Gaulle in 1940, and designed to continue the fight against the Axis powers). It was an awkward moment for the two girls, as neither was quite sure how to approach a perfect stranger and ask him home for dinner. However, as they mingled among the parade crowd, Violette managed to strike up a conversation with Sergeant Major Etienne Szabo. Put at ease by Etienne's friendly demeanour, Violette explained the mission her mother had sent her on, and he graciously accepted her invitation to come for dinner. Etienne had been stationed in Norway when the Germans swept through Belgium and France, and many in his brigade had headed for Britain so that they could fight along with the Free French Forces. Sparks flew immediately between Violette and Etienne, and less than a month after meeting, on 21 August 1940, they were married in Aldershot. Etienne and Violette enjoyed a brief honeymoon and then were separated for more than a year after Etienne was stationed abroad. Szabo was lonely without her husband and waited desperately for his letters to arrive. She found work at a London telephone exchange in order to fill her days, but found it extremely boring and was still convinced she was capable of more important things. In September 1941 Etienne returned to Britain for a brief visit, and Szabo was overjoyed to see her husband. They were reunited for several days and spent a holiday together in Liverpool. While they enjoyed their reunion, Szabo asked Etienne if she could join the Auxiliary Territorial Service (ATS). He did not want his wife to work, but understood

Szabo's desire to keep busy. It was also during this reunion that Szabo became pregnant with her only child – a child whom Etienne would never see. When Etienne returned to his unit, Szabo eagerly enlisted in the ATS. She spent several weeks completing anti-aircraft training and was thrilled with her new assignment. However, shortly into her training she was forced to leave the ATS when she discovered she was pregnant. On 8 June 1942, Szabo gave birth to her daughter, Tania Damaris Désirée Szabo. A few months later, on 24 October 1942, Etienne was killed in action during the Battle of El Alamein in North Africa. Szabo was inconsolable when she got the news.

The Special Operations Executive (SOE) was created in 1940, after the fall of France, and was designed to provide assistance to the Resistance movements in occupied countries. In 1942, approval was given for women to be sent into France. Since all able-bodied French men were expected to be part of the wartime labour force, the Germans would be suspicious of men moving about the countryside, apparently unemployed. Women, however, would not raise these suspicions, and therefore SOE felt that women would be better able to act as couriers (individuals who carried both information and materials) for the wireless operators, saboteurs and intelligence operatives they sent into France, and to organise regional resistance groups. After the birth of her daughter, Szabo was recruited by the SOE. She received a curious summons to report for an interview in London where, most likely due to her knowledge of both France and the French language, Szabo was asked if she would be willing to go into Occupied France to take part in activities designed to undermine the German war effort. Devastated by the death of her husband and looking for a way to strike back at the Germans, Szabo agreed and, after placing her daughter in the care of her family, began training for her role as an SOE operative.

Training, for SOE operatives, was intensive. Candidate agents first attended a preliminary school where they were given a series of physical and psychological tests, designed to identify whether or not they were suitable candidates for espionage work. Szabo completed her preliminary training at Winterfold House in Surrey, and her initial report was satisfactory, stating,

> 27.8.43 A quiet physically tough, self willed girl of average intelligence. Out for excitement and adventure but not entirely frivolous. Has plenty of confidence in herself and gets on well with others. Plucky and persistent in her endeavours. Not easily rattled. In a limited capacity not calling for too much intelligence and responsibility and not too boring she could probably do a useful job, possibly as a courier.[2]

As a result of her first report, Szabo was sent to Scotland in the autumn of 1943, where she was schooled in the use of weapons and explosives, the art of silent killing, how to use codes in radio operation, map and compass work, and basic sabotage. Most female members of SOE were officially assigned to the First Aid Nursing Yeomanry (FANY), which was an all-female branch of the British military. The FANY women filled numerous positions in the British Armed Forces, including that of drivers, hospital workers and clerical staff. It was also a convenient organisation to assign female SOE operatives to, since they couldn't be assigned to any of the regular military services, which were closed to women. It was during training that Szabo met, and became friends with, fellow agent Nancy Wake. Wake had already been heavily involved in Resistance activities back in Vichy France, and had made a daring escape over the mountains into Spain after her activities had made her a target for the Germans. Once in Britain, Wake was very quickly recruited by SOE and she began her training around the same time as Szabo, although they were not, initially, in the same training group. The two women met at an explosives training course and with their vibrant and fun-loving personalities they became great friends and immediate partners in mischief. Wake remembered Szabo fondly, recalling that 'not only was she very beautiful, but she was great fun'.[3] The two women shared many evenings, enjoying the London nightlife, carousing and breaking hearts, and through combined efforts even managed to 'de-pants' an instructor and hoist his trousers up a flagpole! Szabo also developed a relationship with another agent, Harry Peulevé. Peulevé had become acquainted with Szabo in London and fallen deeply in love with her. There is no evidence documenting how Szabo felt about him, but at the very least a strong friendship formed between them. Unfortunately, because of the secrecy of their work, neither could be completely honest with each other, and Peulevé later lamented that their 'pathetic pretence saddened me, especially as our relationship had become extremely intimate. I had to go back to France without being able to tell her, and she also had to go without being able to tell me.'[4]

At this stage of her training there were conflicting reports with regard to Szabo's suitability for covert operations. While she was an excellent shot (the best in her training class), some officers felt that she lacked the right temperament for espionage, and she had some difficulty using codes. Her progress reports from her training officers paint a picture of a highly adventurous and slightly reckless young woman. Szabo's instructors' observations of her potential for use in undercover operations read as follows:

7.9.43 I seriously wonder if this student is suitable for our purpose ... although she works well in the company of others, does not appear to have any initiative or ideals.

21.9.43 Character is difficult to describe: Pleasant personality, sociable, likeable, painstaking, anxious to please, keen ... She is very anxious to carry on with the training but I am afraid it is not with the idea of improving her knowledge but simply because she enjoys the course, the spirit of competition, the novelty of the thing, and being very fit ... must admit she is rather a puzzle.

8.10.43 I have come to the conclusion that this student is tempermentally unsuitable for this work. I consider that owing to her too fatalistic outlook in life ... and the fact that she lacks the ruse, stability and the finesse which is required and that she is too easily influenced; when operating in the field she might endanger the lives of others working with her.[5]

Despite the negative tone of her final report, someone in the SOE had confidence in Szabo. Certainly the Chief Instructor, Major Oliver Brown, thought Szabo had something to offer, for when interviewed in 1992 and asked about his recollections of Szabo, he stated, 'Violette Szabo was marvelous ... but you had to watch her because she was so keen that anything could happen with her ... she was so volatile ... she was a lovely person.'[6] Szabo's final report was ignored and she was recommended for 'finishing school' at Beaulieu (Hampshire). The 'finishing school' was in fact a collection of homes located on the Montagu estate in Beaulieu, which had been requisitioned by SOE as a base for their training operations. Here, recruits were provided with more specific instruction on how to effectively play the part of secret agent, and the security training the agents received at Beaulieu was designed to help agents in fine-tuning their security skills, and to extend the training they had received in Scotland. Szabo was also scheduled for parachute training and earmarked for a position as a courier. Her first parachute jump was a disaster, resulting in a badly sprained ankle that never actually healed properly. However, Szabo finished her training by successfully completing three parachute jumps: one from an aircraft, one from a balloon by day and one from a balloon by night. She received solid marks in her final parachute report, dated 25 February 1944. In April 1944, she was assigned her first mission. Interestingly, her friend Harry Peulevé was working in France at this time and, knowing that Szabo had probably finished her training, had requested that a female courier be sent to him in order to help him in his work. Whether this stemmed from a simple desire to see Szabo again, or the thought that perhaps he might be able to protect her from danger is unclear. Peulevé did say that he was not surprised when Szabo was not assigned to him. He felt that Vera Atkins, one of SOE's most influential figures when it came to the recruitment

acts of sabotage and running escape networks for captured soldiers, downed airmen and refugees. Most sources indicate that Szabo and Liewer were parachuted into France on 5/6 April 1944 but there is at least one source, close to Szabo, who insists that Szabo and Liewer were landed by Lysander. This possibility is credible, since Philippe Liewer was known to hate parachuting! In any event, both Szabo and Liewer landed safely in France. They were met by their reception committee and taken to a safe house where they spent the night. The next day Szabo departed for Paris where she caught a train to Rouen. For weeks, Szabo travelled around the Rouen area, acting as a courier and gathering information about what had happened to the SALESMAN network. Travelling about the area was extremely hazardous as it was teeming with German soldiers. Szabo's beauty attracted the attentions of many of the soldiers and she had to be careful not to speak too much, for although she spoke perfect French, her accent was decidedly English. During her time in France, Szabo discovered that most of the SALESMAN network's members had been arrested and deported to Germany. Under the direction of Liewer, she set about re-establishing contacts between Resistance members. It was imperative that the Resistance resume their activity in this area because of the major railroad marshalling yards located there and because the River Seine, which linked the Atlantic Ocean to Paris, was of extreme strategic importance. A Resistance network needed to be in place for both information gathering (mostly regarding shipping and troop transports) and sabotage purposes. Having done what they could to re-establish the SALESMAN network, Szabo and Liewer returned to Britain on 30 April 1944, both of them pleased with the success of their mission, and Szabo heavily laden down with the Paris fashions she had purchased before she departed!

SOE was extremely impressed with Szabo's performance in the field and she was recommended for a commission as an ensign in the FANY with an increase in pay from £300 to £325 per annum. While awaiting her next assignment she had several weeks to visit her family and spend some time clubbing with her friends in London. Szabo even brought her daughter Tania to the SOE offices on two occasions to show off her beautiful little girl. It was a pleasant time for Szabo but it soon came to an end when she received her summons to report back for duty. A new network, called SALESMAN 2, was to be established in the Haute Vienne (France), and its task was to work in conjunction with the other area networks to disrupt, by sabotage, German transportation and communication systems in coordination with the Allied invasion of Europe (D-Day). The Allied forces, specifically Britain, Canada and the United States, had been planning the invasion of Europe for over two years. They knew they faced formidable German defences, not only in terms of troops and machinery, but also in the form of the Atlantic Wall, an extensive system of coastal fortifications designed to repel any attack on Europe's western coast. Concrete pillboxes housing machine guns and anti-tank guns, minefields and anti-tank obstacles lined the coast of France. The Allies knew that their frontal assault on the beaches would need to be supplemented by as much disruption as possible behind the German lines. Resistance networks were asked to cut telephone lines, in order to undermine the communication between German units and German Army headquarters. The Resistance was also charged with the responsibility of sabotaging railway lines, roads and bridges, to keep reinforcements and supplies from reaching the front-line German troops and to impede any German retreat. Philippe Liewer would be in charge of the new network, Robert Maloubier would be the group's arms instructor, Szabo the group's courier and Jean Claude Guiet would act as the group's wireless operator. Liewer, Maloubier and Szabo were old friends and were excited about the opportunity to work together.

Departing agents were housed at Hassell Hall, Tempsford, up until they flew to France. Hassell Hall was a beautiful country home and it was here that agents received their final briefings and went through their last-minute security checks. Szabo had been given an identity card bearing the name Madame Villeret and her cover story was that she was the widow of an antiques dealer from Nantes. The group was scheduled to depart on 4 June 1944, but poor weather forced a delay. Szabo, Maloubier, Guiet and Liewer spent the next day in Cambridge, relaxing and enjoying a pleasant lunch before returning to the hall, where they spent the rest of the time listening to records, playing cards (blackjack was a favourite) and socialising with fellow agents. Early on the morning of 8 June 1944, one day after the invasion of Europe had begun, Szabo, Robert Maloubier, Philippe Liewer and Jean Claude Guiet parachuted into France near the Sussac area. They had actually flown to France the day before but their plane (a B-24 Liberator) had been forced to turn back as there was no reception committee waiting for them. As the plane returned to England, it passed over the invasion fleet that had set sail for the Normandy beaches. In the windowless plane, Szabo, Maloubier and Guiet had no idea what was taking place beneath them. Liewer had seen the armada from the cockpit of the plane but said nothing to his comrades. Early the next morning Szabo woke them all with the news that the invasion of Europe had begun. Knowing her talent for practical jokes, Maloubier recalls that he and Guiet threw her out of their bedroom and went back to sleep, only to discover upon waking (at noon, no less) that Szabo had been speaking the truth!

After landing in France, Szabo, Guiet, Liewer and Maloubier got into a large car and were driven to a grocer's shop in the village of Sussac, where they were fed and given rooms to sleep in. They were dismayed to discover that almost half of the supplies that were dropped with them had been destroyed, as the parachutes attached to the packages had failed to deploy. There was nothing they could do about that, however, so they quickly turned their focus to their mission, which was to make contact with local Resistance leaders and assist them in organising sabotage activities. The D-Day commanders were relying heavily on the French Resistance to disrupt German communications in the days following the Allied invasion, and the SALESMAN network members were eager to get started. On the morning of 10 June, Liewer gave Szabo her first assignment. She was to make contact with Jacques Poirier, the leader of another Resistance network (DIGGER), in order to arrange a meeting between him and Liewer, so that they could share information and coordinate their two networks' activities. Plans had been made for Szabo to travel by car for the first part of her journey and then to complete the trip by bike. She was accompanied by Jacques Dufour and Jean Bariaud, two members of the French Resistance. Before they departed, Szabo requested a Sten gun, which Philippe Liewer loaded for her. Szabo's request for a gun was a curious one in terms of security measures. Travelling through the French countryside was fraught with peril. German roadblocks were common, and being caught with a weapon would result in her immediate arrest, so she certainly endangered herself with this request. More curious still is the fact that she asked for a Sten gun (a large sub-machine gun) rather than a pistol, which would have been much easier to conceal. However, Robert Maloubier clearly remembers Szabo's loathing of Germans, and her determination to kill as many as she could. Perhaps, consciously or subconsciously, Szabo was seeking such an opportunity.

With her bike strapped to the back of the car, Szabo, Dufour and Bariaud set off on their mission. As they approached the village of Salon-la-Tour they encountered a German roadblock manned by the Second SS Panzer Division Das Reich. The Panzer Division had actually been on its way to Normandy but, on the evening of 9 June 1944, one of the division's battalion commanders (Helmut Kämpfe) was kidnapped by some Maquis (armed Resistance fighters). The soldiers from the Second SS Panzer division fanned out throughout the region searching for Kämpfe, and the roadblock they established at Salon-la-Tour was part of this search. The Germans waved for them to stop, and Dufour waved back, slowing down the car. As both Dufour and Szabo were armed, they decided that stopping for the roadblock was not an option, and Dufour murmured to Szabo, who was beside him in the passenger seat, that she needed to be ready to jump out and run. They stopped the car about 35 m from the roadblock, and the trio leapt from the car, seeking cover in an adjacent wheat field. As the Germans gave chase, both Szabo and Dufour laid down withering machine-gun fire. Bariaud, who had been unarmed, disappeared into the depths of the wheat field. Pursued by heavy fire, Szabo and Dufour managed to make their way through the field to the edge of a forest. At first it looked as though they might have made their escape. They travelled quickly through the field, keeping their heads low so that they presented no targets. However, the Germans soon began raking the field with machine-gun fire, and German infantrymen entered the field en masse. At this point, according to Dufour, Szabo fell to the ground, exhausted. Her clothes were torn and she was bleeding from countless scratches she had sustained from the underbrush. Dufour attempted to carry her, but Szabo told him to go on without her, insisting that someone had to reach Philippe Liewer to warn him of the German presence in the area. Szabo covered Dufour's escape with gunfire until her ammunition ran out. Dufour managed to escape and hid beneath a haystack next to a nearby farmhouse. Szabo was taken into custody by the Germans and was, in fact, brought first to the very farm where Dufour was hiding. According to Dufour (in a statement included in Philippe Liewer's official report of Szabo's arrest), 'Last I know was that, half an hour later, Szabo was brought to that very farm by the Germans; I heard them questioning her as to my whereabouts, and heard her answering, laughing "You can run after him, he is far away by now."'[8]

Another witness, Madame Montinin, who lived in the farmhouse where Dufour hid, recalled that Szabo and Dufour defended themselves like lions. Jacques shot until his last bullet and they had nothing left. The Germans injured the lady on the ankle with a bullet. She couldn't walk. That's when they caught her. A German officer approached and offered her a cigarette. She spat in his face and didn't accept it. She was very brave to do that.[9]

Interestingly, Madame Montinin clearly identifies Szabo as having been struck and wounded by a German bullet, whereas Dufour had no recollection of this. It is possible that Madame Montinin was mistaken. Alternatively, Dufour may simply have been unaware that Szabo had been shot, and so attributed her bleeding, which he did remember, to cuts sustained when hitting the ground to fire at the Germans, or to the branches and vegetation they encountered as they attempted to escape through the wheat field. From the farmhouse Szabo was taken first to Gestapo headquarters and then to Limoges prison. Jacques Dufour, with the help of the Montinin family, managed to escape and returned to Liewer, Maloubier and Guiet early the next morning. The group was devastated to learn of the capture of their friend and plans were immediately made to rescue Szabo. Maloubier contacted the local Resistance to see if they had any contacts within Limoges prison. The information that Maloubier received detailed how Szabo was walked down to Gestapo headquarters (approximately half a mile) every couple of days, under the watch of two guards. Maloubier found a local Resistance member who owned a car, and the plan was for Maloubier and the Resistance driver to pull up in front of Szabo and the two guards while they were en route to Gestapo headquarters. The driver was to snatch

Szabo into the car while Maloubier killed the two guards. Unfortunately, just before the plan was implemented, Szabo was moved to Fresnes prison, outside of Paris. With this move, all hopes for a rescue were gone. The SALESMAN network needed to focus on their assignment of disrupting German transportation and communications so that the Allied armies in Normandy could advance off the beaches. There was simply no time to rescue a lost comrade.

Szabo was held at Fresnes prison, but on several occasions was brought to the infamous Avenue Foch where she was interrogated relentlessly. The buildings located at 82, 84 and 86 Avenue Foch had been commandeered by the Germans when they occupied France. Located in a beautiful residential neighbourhood not far from the Arc de Triomphe, they housed the German counter-intelligence branch of the Gestapo and were used for the imprisonment and interrogation of captured foreign agents. Szabo revealed nothing during her interrogations, refusing to name her Resistance contacts or to explain the purpose of her mission. Torturing captured agents was quite common at Avenue Foch, and the Szabo biography *Carve Her Name with Pride* (R. J. Minney) asserts that Szabo was tortured extensively. However, the book contains a great deal of 'conversation' material that it is doubtful the author could have been privy to, so there is a sense that some of the material is fictionalised to create a better and more dramatic story. Other authors, including Susan Ottaway and former intelligence officer and history professor M. R. D. Foot, have examined witness statements from Szabo's cellmates at Fresnes prison, and can find no conclusive evidence that Szabo was tortured during the interrogation process. Whether or not Szabo was physically tortured, the mental torture she would have suffered from her imprisonment, multiple interrogations, and the daily worry that each day might be her last would certainly have been significant. Szabo definitely left her mark on Avenue Foch, as her name was found written on the wall of cell 45 (one of the interrogation cells) when the premises were searched after the war.

In August of 1944, the decision was made to send Szabo to Ravensbrück concentration camp in Germany, along with fellow SOE agents Denise Bloch and Lilian Rolfe. Bloch, aged twenty-nine, was a French Jewess who had been trained by SOE as a wireless operator and had been working with the CLERGYMAN network near Nantes since early March 1944. She was arrested on 19 June 1944 after a Gestapo raid on the home where she was staying. Rolfe, aged thirty, had been working as a wireless operator for the HISTORIAN network since April 1944. On 31 July 1944, the home she was staying in was raided by the Germans, and Rolfe was arrested. Szabo, Bloch and Rolfe, along with hundreds of other prisoners of war, were loaded aboard a train bound for Germany. As the prisoners lined up, in the crowd Szabo caught a glimpse of her old friend Harry Peulevé, who had been arrested in March. The Germans' decision to move these prisoners was no doubt influenced by the fact that the Allied armies had long since broken through the German defences on the Normandy beaches and were, by August, closing in on Paris. At some point during the trip the train was bombed by the Royal Air Force (RAF). The train stopped and, leaving the prisoners on board, the German guards exited the train to machine-gun the planes. Many of the prisoners were in a panic, fearing the bombs might hit the train, and dozens were suffering from dehydration, as they had been packed into the cars with no food or water in the scorching August heat. Amid the exploding bombs and machine-gun fire, Szabo, Bloch and Rolfe crawled along the floor of the train to bring water to the suffering prisoners. Harry Peulevé witnessed this act, and declared, 'I shall never forget that moment ... I felt very proud that I knew her. She looked so pretty, despite her shabby clothes and her lack of make-up – she was full of good cheer.'[10] Another agent, Forest Yeo-Thomas, was also impressed by the bravery of Szabo, Bloch and Rolfe, stating, 'Through the din, they shouted words of encouragement to us, and seemed quite unperturbed. I can only express my unbounded admiration for them and words are so inadequate that I cannot hope to say what I felt then and still feel now.'[11]

Taken from the train, as the track had been heavily damaged by the bombing, both the male and female prisoners were loaded into heavily armed trucks and driven to Gestapo headquarters at Châlons-sur-Marne. The prisoners were allowed to wash in a local fountain, and conversed with each other as their captors received further instructions regarding the transport of the prisoners. They spent the night sleeping in stables, with the male prisoners separated from the females. The German guards had orders to shoot anyone who tried to cross over. Still, Peulevé managed to exchange some whispered words with Szabo. He recalled,

We spoke of old times and we told each other our experiences in France. Bit by bit everything was unfolded – her life in Fresnes, her interviews at the Avenue Foch ... She was in a cheerful mood. Her spirits were high. She was confident of victory and was resolved on escaping no matter where they took her.[12]

The next morning the prisoners were transported to Metz and then on to a camp at Saarbrücken. Szabo was kept there for several days, and was briefly reunited with fellow agent Yvonne Baseden. The two women had a brief opportunity to chat, but Szabo was soon loaded aboard a cattle car to be transferred to Ravensbrück. Baseden would eventually follow Szabo to Ravensbrück, but she never saw her colleague again.

Szabo, Rolfe and Bloch arrived at the camp on 22 August 1944. Ravensbrück was the only major Nazi camp designed specifically for women. Opened in 1939 and located approximately 90 km north of Berlin, the camp had a terrifying reputation. Prisoners in the camp existed under horrific conditions, and murders occurred daily, as a result of starvation, beating, torture, hanging and shooting. Medical experimentation on the prisoners was also commonplace. After arriving at Ravensbrück, Szabo, Rolfe and Bloch were sent to several different work camps. In September, they were shipped to Torgau (193 km south of Ravensbrück) where they performed factory work. Conditions there were bearable, and witnesses recall that Szabo was very cheerful and was planning to escape. She actually managed to get hold of a key to one of the camp gates, but had to throw it away when someone informed on her. In late October 1944, Szabo, Bloch and Rolfe were relocated to a camp in Königsberg. Conditions here were dreadful, and the women worked long hours in the cold, assisting in the construction of an airfield. One of Szabo's fellow prisoners wrote frequently to Violette's parents after the war, and, after seeing the movie *Carve Her Name with Pride*, wrote a letter to them stating,

> You will understand why I feel shocked when I see pictures of the film on Violette with the women in the camp wearing so much clothes – my poor darling had only one blue silk frock, a fringe from hem to her knees and short sleeved, this is the way we were clothed to face a Prussian winter.[13]

The inadequate food, squalid living conditions and hard labour, clearing brush and trees, made life miserable for Szabo, but she still managed to make quite a few friends while she was imprisoned. Survivors remembered her fondly. In early 1945 the three British SOE agents were recalled from the work camp at Königsberg and returned to Ravensbrück. They were housed in the punishment block where they had no contact with other prisoners, but rumours spread quickly that the women had returned to the camp. Lilian Rolfe and Denise Bloch were both very ill by this time, and only Szabo was able to walk. One evening, sometime during late January or early February, the three women were summoned from their cells. They were led to a courtyard known as execution alley. Holding hands, the three condemned women knelt down as the order of their execution was read out. One by one they were executed by a single gunshot through the back of the neck, and their bodies were immediately stripped and cremated. Violette Szabo was twenty-three years old.

After the war, survivors from Ravensbrück talked

admiringly of Szabo's bravery, as did her colleagues in the SOE. The three men who accompanied Szabo on her last mission (Robert Maloubier, Philippe Liewer and Jean Claude Guiet) all survived the war. On 28 January 1947, seven-year-old Tania Szabo accepted the George Cross on behalf of her late mother. The medal was presented by King George VI at Buckingham Palace. Three years later, Tania, wearing the George Cross, was presented with the Croix de Guerre (a French military decoration awarded to those who had performed a heroic act in combat with the enemy) by the French ambassador. A plaque mounted outside the Violette Szabo Museum in Herefordshire, England, reads as follows:

> This plaque is placed
> as an evergreen tribute to
> VIOLETTE SZABO, G.C.
> British Secret Agent
> Born 26th June 1921
> Executed by the Gestapo
> at Ravensbrück during 1945
> In deep appreciation of her outstanding
> courage in England's hour of need.
> Violette spent many happy holidays here
> at 'Cartref' with her Aunt and Uncle
> Mr. & Mrs. H. Lucas and family.
> R.I.P. Violette
> 'Carve her name with pride'
>   Rosemary E. Rigby, 1988

The story of Violette Szabo has continued to capture the

imagination of thousands of people. In 1958, a British film, *Carve Her Name with Pride*, based on R. J. Minney's Szabo biography of the same name, was released. It starred Virginia McKenna as Violette, and former SOE Chief Instructor Major Oliver Brown stated in a 1992 interview that 'McKenna portrayed her absolutely exactly'.[14] Tania Szabo was raised by her grandparents and moved to Australia in 1951. She returned to England in 1963 and now lives in Wales. She has written her own account of her mother's life, *Young Brave and Beautiful*, which proved to be so popular that it is currently sold out. Tania maintains the Violette Szabo, George Cross website. In 2009, a sculpture of Szabo was unveiled opposite London's Houses of Parliament on the Albert Embankment, and Szabo's story is on permanent display in the Szabo Room at the Jersey War Tunnels.

2

Nancy Wake (1912–2011)
Code Name:
Hélène/Witch/The White Mouse

Bawdy, irreverent, brazen and adventurous, Nancy Wake was the Allies' most decorated servicewoman of the Second World War. Like a steam engine, Nancy roared through life with a personality so big that a meeting with her was impossible to forget. Not exactly a desirable trait for undercover work, where the idea is to maintain a low profile! Yet everything about Nancy was magnified: her personality, her sense of humour, her thirst for adventure and, most importantly, her courage. Nancy Wake was one of those few individuals who were truly larger than life and, although she was nicknamed 'The White Mouse', it would have been more apt to compare her to a lion.

Nancy Grace Augusta Wake entered the world on 30 August 1912. She was born in Wellington, New Zealand, to Charles Augustus and Ella Rosieur Wake, and was the youngest of six children. Her father, a journalist, moved his family to Sydney, Australia, when Nancy was two, and subsequently abandoned them, leaving Nancy's mother to raise six children on her own. Nancy was a handful, even as a child, and she chafed against her mother's strict religious parenting, the rules and restrictions of school, and the lack of glamour and adventure that she associated with being the youngest child in a large family that struggled to make ends meet. Her confidence and adventurous personality were evident early on, and she ran away from home twice as a young girl. By the age of sixteen she had landed herself a position as a trainee nurse at a small healthcare facility in a remote gold-mining town. Amused by her job, Nancy still longed to spread her wings and discover what the rest of world had to offer. After working for two years as a nurse, she returned to Sydney and took a job with a Dutch shipping company. Wake arrived home from work one night and discovered a letter from her mother's sister. Wake's aunt had been a bit of a rebel, too, and had also run away in her teens. Perhaps feeling a sense of affinity for Nancy, the aunt wrote that she was sending Wake £200 to help her make a start in life. This windfall was all the encouragement Wake needed. As she was only eighteen, she lied about her age to get a passport (you needed to be twenty-one), booked herself a first-class ticket, and in December 1932 boarded a ship in Sydney Harbour that was destined for Vancouver, Canada. From there, it was on to New York.

Wake had a blast in Prohibition-era New York. She claimed to have never drunk so much in her life, and spent her time there carousing through speakeasies and imbibing bathtub gin. The glittering New York nightlife suited her and she hated to leave, but her spirit of adventure was tugging at her and she knew she needed to get to Europe before her money ran out. She booked passage on a ship bound for England, and upon landing she found herself a room in a London boarding house and enrolled in a journalism course. Wake felt that this would be the perfect career for her and would allow her to combine both work and travel. From the speakeasies of New York to the pub crawls of London, Wake soon developed a close circle of friends and had an active social life. Money was tight but Wake was ingenious at finding ways to have a good time. She also completed her journalism course and was invited for a job interview for a position covering news in the Middle East. Wake lied easily, saying that she had been to the Middle East many times and could even write in Egyptian (neither were true). Her interviewer was amazed to discover such a qualified candidate and offered Wake a trial position as a freelance reporter based in Paris, from where she could easily travel to cover news stories throughout Europe and the Middle East. Upon accepting the position, Wake was ecstatic at her good fortune and was completely unaware that she was about to experience, first-hand, both the best and worst of humankind.

Wake was twenty-two when she came to Paris in 1934. She embraced life in the French capital, as she had in New York and London, and immediately found herself swept up into the city's gay social whirl. By writing articles and selling them to various press agencies, she managed to eke out a good enough living to pay her rent, provide for frequent nights out on the town and allow her to travel the French countryside in search of good stories and good times. Wake was determined to become a true Parisienne, frequenting French cafés, dressing as elegantly as she could afford to, and even purchasing a small wire-haired terrier that she named Picon, as she had quickly observed that most stylish French women had a small dog as one of their principal accessories! She also made a concerted effort to learn the

French language, although in typical Wake style she recalled, 'I never worried too much about all that bloody feminine/ masculine stuff, all the *le* this and *la* that – it would give you the shits – but it wasn't too long before I could communicate what I wanted to say, and I got better from there.'[1]

Working as a journalist, Wake soon realised that she needed to become much better informed about politics. She read voraciously on the subject, and began attending rallies and protests to better understand the issues about which she was being asked to write. She also watched with apprehension as Adolf Hitler and his Nazi Party took control of Germany. Rumours about the harsh National Socialist policies trickled into France through the refugees who were attempting to escape the oppressive regime. Wake and a group of her journalist friends decided to see for themselves what the Nazis were capable of. The group took a trip to the Austrian capital of Vienna, where the party was gaining strength. There, Wake witnessed Nazi party members persecuting and abusing Austrian Jews on numerous occasions. Wake was horrified by what she saw, and explained, 'It was in Vienna that I formed my opinion of the Nazis. I resolved there and then that if I ever had the chance I would do anything, however big or small, stupid or dangerous, to try and make things more difficult for their rotten party.'[2]

She also had occasion to visit Berlin, the German capital, later in 1934, and saw Jewish shops defaced with red paint, the stores themselves looted and the shopkeepers whipped. Filled with revulsion, Wake returned to Paris, but, while she enjoyed her carefree and fun-filled lifestyle, the memories of what she had witnessed stayed with her. When war broke out in France, Nancy Wake was prepared to fight.

Wake continued to enjoy all that Paris had to offer despite the political upheavals that were taking place throughout Europe. As Germany marched into the Rhineland in 1936 before annexing Austria in 1938, and the Spanish Civil War raged just south of France from 1936 to 1939, Wake worked steadily as a journalist, surrounding herself with friends and sharing the company of Picon, to whom she was devoted. With everything that was happening in Europe, there was certainly no shortage of news stories to be covered, and Wake was constantly on the move. Work did not preclude her from having an active social life, however, and, after a series of casual affairs, Wake met and fell in love with a wealthy Frenchman named Henri Fiocca. Despite the fact that Fiocca's family did not care for her and viewed her as a gold-digger, Wake and Fiocca made plans to marry. In July 1939, Wake had decided to resign her position with the news agency. Her plans were to travel to Paris to tender her resignation, pack her belongings and lease her flat so that she could move south to Marseille to live with Fiocca. She also wanted to slim down before her wedding, so as soon as she tied up her affairs in Paris she boarded a ship to Britain, in late August 1939, in order to spend some time at a health spa. Her leisurely spa vacation was rudely interrupted, however. By the time she had arrived in London, Germany had invaded Poland, and France and Britain had declared war on Germany. Wake, keen to take on the Nazis, cancelled her health spa reservation and reported immediately to a London recruiting office to offer her services. She was quite insulted when the recruiting officer suggested that she might find a canteen to serve in! Disgusted that the British were not more interested in her services, Wake quickly booked a ticket back to France. She married Henri Fiocca in Marseille in November 1939, and was now provided with a life of luxury. The couple had a fabulous apartment overlooking the harbour in Marseille, they travelled extensively and Wake totally immersed herself in the sophisticated life. Although war had been declared, nothing much seemed to be happening, and during this period of 'Phoney War' Wake enjoyed her new role as a wealthy newly-wed. This idyllic existence was about to change, however, because in May of 1940 Germany invaded France.

Henri Fiocca had received his call-up papers for the army early in 1940, and he departed for his posting (an unknown destination) in March of that year. Shortly after, in May, the Germans invaded the Low Countries (the Netherlands and Belgium). Wake, always a woman of action, responded to the German aggression by taking the vehicle Fiocca had left her and turning it into an ambulance. She immediately joined a volunteer ambulance unit and drove to the north of France to provide medical assistance to the troops and refugees in that region. By June, however, the Germans had swept through the Netherlands, Belgium and France, and France officially asked for an armistice with Germany on 16 June. The terms of the armistice were harsh and dealt a crushing blow to the morale of the French population. Three-fifths of their country fell under German occupation, including the same proportion of the Atlantic ports. French Jews and Germans who had sought asylum in France were to be turned over to German officials and all French soldiers captured by the Germans were to remain incarcerated until the end of the war. The French were also expected to incur the cost of paying for the German occupation force. Following the armistice, France was separated into an Occupied Zone and a Free Zone where the Germans still exerted control but their presence was slightly less noticeable. The Free Zone became known as Vichy France since it was governed from the city of Vichy. With the French army defeated and demobilised, Fiocca returned from the war and joined his wife in their apartment in Marseille, which was located inside the so-called 'Free Zone'. Wake, devoted to her adopted country of France, refused to tolerate anyone who supported the Germans or the Vichy government, and adjusted her social circle accordingly. She wanted to be able to speak freely about her views on the Occupation, and made sure that she surrounded herself with people she was sure she could trust. Wake also caught wind of the existence of emerging Resistance groups. These early Resistance groups consisted of French men and women who were determined to make the Occupation as unpleasant as possible for the Germans. Unlawfully flying the French flag, defacing German propaganda posters, sabotaging German military equipment, and establishing escape lines out of France (for refugees, escaped British prisoners of war, downed British and Polish pilots, etc.) were all ways that the French Resistance attempted to continue the fight against the Germans. Well known for her anti-German and anti-Vichy sentiments, it wasn't long before Wake was approached to assist in some Resistance-type activities.

Wake's position as the wife of a wealthy industrialist allowed her many privileges that were denied to the rest of the French population. She was able to travel extensively, and could afford both luxury and everyday items that were becoming more expensive and difficult to find under the

German Occupation. Wake made friends with a number of British prisoners who had been interned at a fort in Marseille after the fall of France. She used her money to supply the prisoners with a radio, cigarettes and food parcels, so that their confinement was a little more tolerable. On her travels throughout France, she carried papers (which included not only messages but forged identity cards for people whom the Resistance were helping to escape from France) for French Resistance groups, and even opened up her own apartment and her chalet in Névache to hide individuals who were on the run from the Germans or the French Milice. The French Milice were a secret police, similar to the Gestapo, but perhaps even more terrifying since they were French and were turning on their own countrymen. Wake hated the Milice as much as she hated the Germans, describing them as 'a small army of vicious Frenchmen dedicated to ferreting out members of the Resistance and slaughtering them ... arrogant, savagely cruel, treacherous and sadistic ... They had absolutely no compassion for any of their compatriots who did not support their beliefs.'[3]

Wake teamed up with a Scottish officer, Ian Garrow, who had escaped from internment at the fort in Marseille, and had established an escape line for Allied (at this point mostly British and Canadian) prisoners. She worked as his courier and helped to scout out safe houses for the prisoners between Cannes and Toulon. Fiocca provided her with the money to purchase food and ration cards for the prisoners. Things seemed to be going quite well until suddenly Garrow was arrested. Wake did not abandon her friend, sending him food and letters in prison, and even paid for a lawyer to plead his case before the Vichy courts. When she discovered that Garrow was being sent to the Meauzac concentration camp, she initiated a plan to break him out. Wake visited Garrow every week and finally made contact with a guard who was agreeable to taking a bribe in order to help Garrow escape. The money for the bribe would, of course, come from Henri Fiocca's deep pockets. After weeks of planning, a guard's uniform was secreted into the prison. On 8 December 1942, Garrow donned the uniform and joined a line of guards who were leaving the prison at the end of their shift. The Resistance was waiting to pick him up in a car, and over the next several days Garrow made his way to a safe house in Toulouse where Wake was able to meet with him. A few days later, Garrow made his escape over the mountains into Spain, eventually making his way all the way to Britain. Wake was overjoyed at their success and determined to continue Garrow's work.

Wake's activities did not go unnoticed by the Germans or the Vichy police, however. They knew that a woman fitting Wake's description was a key member of the Resistance, but their inability to actually catch her doing anything criminal led to the Germans nicknaming her The White Mouse. Discovering that the Germans had given her a nickname delighted Wake no end. Her phones were tapped, her mail was monitored and she was followed, but somehow she managed to avoid actually incriminating herself. However, she felt that the authorities were drawing ever closer. After the Allied landings in Vichy-controlled North Africa, many of the French soldiers stationed there joined the Allied forces. The Germans, fearing an Allied invasion of southern France, occupied the Free Zone in November of 1942. With the increased German military presence Wake knew that her days were numbered. The decision was made for Wake to attempt to escape to Britain via a route over the Pyrenees (the same one Garrow had taken), a mountain range that forms a natural border between France and Spain. She was distraught at having to leave both Fiocca and her little dog Picon but realised that she would become a prisoner of the Gestapo if she stayed. Six times she attempted to cross the Pyrenees into Spain, but the heavily patrolled border proved a formidable obstacle. After several months she finally succeeded. She arrived in Britain in the middle of June 1943 and rented a small flat in London. She hoped desperately that her husband would soon join her, and while she waited she became dreadfully bored, missing the action and intrigue that working with the Resistance had brought into her life. After several weeks spent socialising with old friends, Wake applied to the Free French Forces, an army of Frenchmen organised by Charles de Gaulle, who refused to recognise France's surrender to the Germans and who had vowed to continue the fight against Germany. Wake hoped that the Free French would be able to send her back into France to continue her work against the Germans. To her shock, Colonel Passy, the Free French officer who interviewed her, declined her application, for reasons that were never made clear. Indignant that the French were not interested in her services, Wake asked one of her British officer friends to put her in touch with the Special Operations Executive (SOE). SOE called her for an interview and were favourably impressed. They knew all about her work in Marseille and held her in very high esteem. Wake was recommended for training as an SOE operative and assigned to the First Aid Nursing Yeomanry (FANY).

Training Nancy Wake would prove to be an interesting experience for all concerned. She was first sent to a training school just outside of London, where she had the opportunity to meet Colonel Maurice Buckmaster, who was the head of SOE's 'F' Section. The two hit it off immediately and, although not everyone was a Buckmaster fan, Wake described him as 'a lovely man, an Englishman of the old school ... and I loved him. He was a gentleman, and he really cared for each and every one of us.'[4]

Wake thought less highly of her first phase of training, however; during this stage potential recruits were screened, both in terms of their psychology and in their overall aptitude for undercover work. Wake was quite disgusted with the whole arrangement, finding the obstacle course confusing, the task of searching for imaginary hidden papers quite ridiculous and the standard psychiatric ink blot test a complete waste of time. She was convinced that she had failed every test she was put through, but she must have done something right as she was passed on for six more weeks of training in Scotland. Before she left, however, Wake managed to have words with one of the most influential people within SOE, which almost cost her the FANY commission she had been given. The conducting officer for the course, radio expert Denis Rake, had become a good friend of Wake's. His openness about his homosexuality was off-putting for many but Wake accepted him and quite enjoyed his company. One afternoon, Nancy returned from lunch to Welbeck House, where she and the other recruits were staying, and walked in on an argument between Rake and one of the other female recruits. Wake attempted to mind her own business, but as the voices rose and expletives began to fly she found herself in the thick of things. The female recruit was furious with Rake and insisted she was filing a report against him. Then she demanded that Wake act as a witness to Rake's rudeness during their altercation. Wake did not want to be drawn into the conflict, and refused, which further enraged the other recruit. Knowing that Nancy liked to drink, the woman complained to Selwyn Jepson, the man in charge of recruiting SOE agents, that Wake was a drunk, and accused her of not being willing to support her accusation against Denis Rake. Jepson responded to the female agent's complaint by calling a meeting with Wake to question her about her drinking and about her unwillingness to act as a witness for her fellow female agent. Wake was furious that she had been drawn into a conflict in which she had no interest, and took offence at the way Jepson spoke to her. Once he had finished, an exasperated Wake basically told him 'what he could do and where he could put it'.[5] Jepson, shocked by her response and unwilling to be spoken to that way by any recruit, fired her on the spot, while Wake, extremely disappointed (but not remorseful enough to apologise), stormed out. She returned to her flat in London where she received a telegram ordering her to return her FANY uniform to SOE. Fed up, Wake decided to once again offer her services to the Free French, and placed a call to SOE headquarters to tell them 'they could have their bloomin' uniform back, but only if that Jepson came to pick it up himself and apologise to her first'.[6] News of Wake's firing soon reached the uppermost echelons of SOE. Buckmaster, who was very fond of Wake, interceded on her behalf, and somehow managed to smooth things over. SOE rehired her, and scheduled her for the next available training course in Scotland.

Wake's new training group consisted entirely of men. They were housed at Inverie Bay in northern Scotland, and were provided with extensive instruction in the use of explosives, grenades and weaponry. Wake had never held a gun before and found this type of training thoroughly enjoyable. Unlike the psychological tests she had done in her first round of training, she actually saw the skills she was learning in Scotland as eminently useful and not a waste of her time. So thoroughly did she enjoy the course that she actually began to worry about the possibility that her report card may not be good enough for her to continue with training. While she worked reasonably diligently at her training exercises, she was by no means a star pupil and she did have a tendency to engage in mischief. Determined to find out how well (or poorly) she was doing, Wake decided to exercise some of her training in covert operations and sneak a peek at what her report looked like. While the office clerk's back was turned, she used plasticine to make an impression of the office key. Then, later that evening, she posted a friend as a lookout (promising to read his report as payment) and broke into the office where the reports were kept. She was pleased with what she read, seeing no negative comments and discovering that her instructors had written that she was 'good for morale'![7] From Scotland, Wake moved on to Ringway (Manchester) for her parachute training and then to Beaulieu (Hampshire) for security training. She learned how to travel with false identity cards, how to perform surveillance, how to recruit civilians for Resistance work and how to deal with police interrogations. Wake also managed to inject some of her bawdy humour into these training exercises. Two of her more successful pranks included attaching a condom to the back of one instructor and, with fellow SOE agent Violette Szabo, hoisting another instructor's pants up a flagpole! Training soon came to an end, however, and Wake was assigned her first mission.

Assigned the code name Hélène and the cover name of Madame Andrée, Wake parachuted into the Auvergne region of France on 31 April 1944. The flight over the Channel to France aboard a Liberator aircraft was not an easy journey for Wake. Hung-over after a raucous night out to celebrate her impending departure, Wake spent most of the flight fighting off the urge to throw up her Spam dinner in her oxygen mask. Her nausea aside, she certainly made an impression on both her flight crew and her reception committee. In irrepressible Wake fashion, she combined her army-issue overalls and tin hat with silk stockings, high heels and a camel-hair coat. She landed with another SOE operative, Major John Farmer, and their instructions were to link up with the local Resistance, and organise them so that they could both disrupt German lines of communication and launch acts of sabotage against the Germans in coordination with Allied landings in Normandy. Unfortunately, Maurice Southgate, who ran the STATIONER circuit that Wake and Farmer were supposed to join, was arrested before they could make contact. Worse still, their radio operator, Wake's old conducting officer Denis Rake, had refused to be parachuted into France with them, demanding to be landed by Lysander instead. He was landed in France, but had taken off with a boyfriend for the first several days he was there, and Wake and Farmer had no idea where he was. They finally made contact with a local Resistance group, run by a man named Gaspard, but quickly discovered their presence was not welcome. Gaspard made it clear he was unwilling to work with the British and was not interested in any help that Wake and Farmer could provide. The fact that they did not even have a radio operator made the pair even less appealing to him. Stunned by their cool reception, Wake and Farmer went outside to discuss the turn of events, and happened to overhear the Resistance men discussing the fact that the SOE agents were probably carrying a lot of money and that perhaps one of them should seduce Wake, steal her money and kill her that evening. Wake was livid, and confronted the man, creating quite a scene. Gaspard decided to rid himself of both Wake and Farmer by passing them along to another Resistance group run by a man named Henri Fournier. Here they met with a much warmer reception, and Fournier graciously offered them hotel accommodation in a remote village called Lieutadès where they could await the arrival of their radio operator.

Denis Rake resurfaced in the middle of May, making contact with Wake as she was driving by the Lieutadès cemetery. Although Wake and Farmer were furious with Rake (as they were quite certain that he had been off following some amorous adventure), they were also extremely glad to see him. Moreover, Fournier was ecstatic that his group would now be in radio contact with London. Lists of explosives and weapons they wanted were coded by Wake and transmitted by Rake. Drop sites were scouted, and Wake and her team manned the sites from 10 p.m. until 4 a.m., signalling to the aircraft, retrieving the containers, unpacking them and distributing their contents to the Resistance. Wake was also in charge of the group's finances. She decided which

Resistance groups were to receive the arms and explosives as well as monetary support. Her position was an extremely powerful one and the various Resistance groups competed to win her favour. Even Gaspard and his men, who had been savaged by a German attack on their positions in late May, now came to Wake for supplies. However, not all of the air-dropped packages were earmarked for the Resistance. Occasionally parcels were dropped that contained personal items for the agents. Wake's always contained Elizabeth Arden products, speciality teas, chocolates and letters from friends.

The large group of Resistance fighters in the Auvergne region eventually attracted the attention of the Germans, and many small battles took place. It was during one of these firefights that a Frenchman named Roger, who had earlier infiltrated the Resistance working as a Gestapo spy, was captured. Several Resistance men interrogated him rather brutally, and Roger confessed to being responsible for the arrest and torture of a number of Resistance members. His confession was recorded and Wake took it for transmission back to London. Roger was subsequently executed by the Resistance and buried in the forest. Wake was uncomfortable with the torture the man received, but conceded,

There is a lot to be said for the proverb 'an eye for an eye', and when all is said and done Roger was only paying for some of the abominable treatment meted out to his victims. Torture is horrible. But before any outsiders form an opinion they should study both sides of the story closely.[8]

unpacking containers up at one of the drop sites. As she crawled into bed she was startled by the sound of gunfire. The group's lookouts arrived and announced that the whole area surrounding their mountain hideout was ringed by over 22,000 German troops who were supported by tanks, heavy artillery and aircraft. Wake, Farmer and Rake packed quickly and joined the larger group of Resistance fighters who had taken up positions on the plateau. As the Resistance worked feverishly to hold back the German onslaught, Rake attempted to contact London via radio, and Wake put all the weapons received the night before into working condition and drove them out to the Resistance's outlying positions. Eventually a response from London was received and the whole group was ordered to withdraw from the area.

Wake travelled for two days with virtually no food or water. She and a group of about thirty Resistance men eventually reached the outskirts of the town of Saint-Santin where they decided to set up headquarters. Denis Rake joined them a few days later but he had buried his radio and destroyed his codes, so the group was without contact with London. This was a dreadful blow, since there was no way to arrange for supply drops or to receive orders. Through a local contact, Wake heard that there was a Free French wireless operator located approximately 200 km away. She volunteered to travel by bicycle in order to meet with him. Many of the group counselled against this plan as roadblocks had been set up across the entire region. Moreover, the Germans had declared that all the identity cards of local citizens had to be exchanged, under German supervision, for new ones. Obviously Wake could not participate in the exchange so all of her papers were now invalid. To travel such a distance without the proper identification was extremely hazardous. Without radio contact with London, however, the group was in serious trouble, and there appeared to be no better plan than Wake's. She followed a circuitous route and was forced to take many detours to avoid German troops and roadblocks. After a great deal of difficulty, she finally found a Resistance group that was organised by the Free French, and their radio operator agreed to send a message to Colonel Buckmaster at SOE on Wake's behalf. Exhausted, Wake forced herself back onto her bicycle for the long trip home and returned to Saint-Santin a mere seventy-two hours after she had left. Her legs were on fire and it took her days to recover, but, when asked about her proudest moment of the war, Wake always said, 'The bike ride.'[10]

Once Wake was able to travel again, she and her group moved north into a region under the command of Henri Tardivat. Tardivat set the group up in an area just outside of Ygrande, close to a field that could be used as a drop site. Wake was extremely happy in her new situation. She had great respect for Tardivat (Tardi, as she called him) and was impressed by his well-run group of Resistance saboteurs. Ambushes were one of Tardivat's specialities and Wake joined him on countless missions, attacking German convoys that were heading towards the Normandy front. Wake and her colleagues favoured roads that ran through thickly wooded areas, where they could line the road with bombs and run a string from the trigger to their hiding spot. When the convoy approached, they would detonate the bombs and strafe the Germans with gunfire, forcing them to evacuate their vehicles. Tardivat insisted that there be no sustained contact with the enemy, and on his signal the group would simply blend back into the darkness. London had received Wake's message from the Free French radio operator and dispatched not only supplies but also a new radio operator, who would work in conjunction with Denis Rake. Wake continued to be in charge of the group's finances and the distribution of arms, and she was not above using her powerful position to secure herself some creature comforts. Sick and tired of sleeping on the damp ground with her compatriots, Wake decided she required indoor sleeping quarters, and she figured a bus with two facing rear seats would be just the thing. She had already received a mattress from Tardivat, so when he requested an additional shipment of Bren guns she was more than happy to accommodate, as long as he could provide her with the bus she wanted. Tardivat and his Resistance men set up a roadblock and stopped every bus that passed by until they found one with two facing rear seats. The unfortunate bus passengers had a long walk ahead of them, but Tardivat received his guns, and Wake now had a bedroom to call her own!

Wake's group was constantly on the move and continued to come under German attack. They in turn attacked German patrols, and continued to ambush convoys of food that were being sent to feed both German civilians and the troops at the front. Wake maintained contact with all of the Resistance groups in the area, travelling extensively to provide them with money and arms, and also searching for potential drop sites where the group could receive their deliveries. She also continued to work closely with Tardivat on his sabotage missions. They blew up numerous bridges and attacked hundreds of convoys. Wake discovered she loved using the tripwire technique, which involved stretching a wire, attached to explosives, between two trees on each side of the road. The first vehicle in each convoy would blow up, causing damage to those behind it and blocking the road so that the rest of the group would come to a standstill. One of her most exciting missions was the attack she participated in on Gestapo headquarters in Montluçon. Tardivat came up with the plan, and spent days monitoring the headquarters and recording how many sentries were on duty, when the shift changes occurred and where the defences were situated. His plan called for one group to implement the actual attack and for another to cover the escape of the attackers. Wake was over the moon to discover she was to be included in the attacking group. Tardivat, Wake and fourteen others drove into Montluçon in four separate cars, and arrived in front of Gestapo headquarters at 12.25 p.m. As Wake described it, she 'entered the building by the back door, raced up the stairs, opened the first door along the passage way and threw in my grenades, closed the door and ran like hell back to my car which was ready to make a quick getaway'.[11] The getaway was not quite as quick as Wake had hoped, as the people of Montluçon crowded the streets, cheering for them, but blocking the cars in the process. Some frantic horn blowing cleared the way, and Wake and her colleagues made their escape. Wake seemed to thrive on danger, and there was plenty of it – not always in the form of German soldiers, either. Because of her powerful position, she was bound to make enemies, and one afternoon a Resistance fighter from a group that Wake had refused to arm decided he was going to kill her. Fortunately for Wake, the man had been drinking heavily. As her car approached a small village, the man, who was waiting for her, pulled out a grenade and the grenade pin. All of his drinking had slowed his reflexes, however, and he held it in his hand too long. The grenade exploded, taking his hand with it. When his intent was revealed to Wake, she refused to feel sorry for him and, from that point on, she always travelled with a bodyguard.

Paris was liberated on 25 August 1944, and the Germans pulled out of Vichy in September. Wake and her group immediately travelled to Vichy where Wake was stunned by the news that her beloved husband Henri Fiocca was dead. He had been arrested by the Gestapo in May 1943, and held in prison until he died five months later. Fiocca had been tortured extensively, but had refused to reveal the whereabouts of his cherished wife. For that act of courage, he ultimately paid with his life. Wake was devastated by the news and, while she was never one to second-guess herself, she was the first to admit, 'I will go to my grave regretting that. Henri was the love of my life.'[12] Wake did discover that her little dog Picon had survived, and she took some consolation from that happy reunion.

After the war, Wake was awarded numerous medals for her work in France, including the George Medal (from Britain); the Croix de Guerre with palm and bar, the Croix de Guerre with star, the Médaille de la Résistance, the Chevalier de la Légion d'honneur, and the Officier de la Légion d'honneur (from France); and the Medal of Freedom (from the United States). She worked for the British Foreign Office, attached to the embassies in Paris and Prague, until 1949 when she returned to Australia and tried her hand at politics. She ran as a Liberal Party candidate in the Australian federal election of 1949 but was defeated. Wake returned to England in 1951 and took a position as an officer in the Intelligence

Department of the British Air Ministry. She left this post in 1958, shortly after marrying John Forward, a former RAF pilot who had spent much of the war in a German POW camp. Her new husband convinced her that their combined pensions would go further in Australia, so the two returned there in 1959. Although she dabbled, unsuccessfully, in politics one more time, Wake spent the majority of her days playing golf, travelling and being a homemaker. She published her autobiography, *The Autobiography of the Woman the Gestapo Called the White Mouse*, in 1985, and soon after that she and Forward purchased a flat in Port Macquarie where they intended to live out their final years. Wake's husband died in 1997, and in 2001, at the age of eighty-nine, Wake sold her flat in Australia and returned to Britain. Australia had lost its appeal for her, and she resented the fact that the Australian government had never invited her to march in any military parades; nor had they recognised her war service with any sort of medal, always asserting that her service had not been as part of the Australian military. In typical Wake form, she announced, just as she was leaving Australia, that 'I'm hoping to find some old friends in town … I'm heading for the Special Forces Club in Knightsbridge to have a bloody good drink.'[13]

Wake took up residence at the Stafford Hotel in London, her stay funded by the sale of her medals, which fetched a price of £60,000. Following a heart attack in 2003, Wake moved into the Royal Star & Garter Home for ex-servicemen. A year later, the Australian government finally recognised Wake's war service by awarding her the Companion of the Order of Australia. New Zealand followed suit in 2006, and awarded her the RSA Badge in Gold. In old age, Nancy

Wake maintained much of the spark she possessed as a young woman, and had lost none of her sense of humour. While chatting with a reporter about the arrangements she had made with regard to her eventual death, she stated, 'I'm going to be cremated and have my ashes flown over the mountains where I fought alongside all those men. And if there is such a person as St Peter, I'm going to make it easy for him: I'm going to plead guilty on all counts.'[14]

Nancy Wake passed away on 7 August 2011 at the age of ninety-eight. In March 2013, at a ceremony held in a wooded area just outside the village of Verneix, Montluçon, France, Nancy Wake's ashes were scattered throughout the forest; the service was attended by two current FANY members, the Head of the Australian Defence Staff, the Australian military attaché from Paris and many others. Even in death, Wake's vibrant personality shone through and, in keeping with her penchant for an early morning gin and tonic, a lively drinks reception was held, as per her request, at the mayor's office, following the ceremony.

Noor Inayat Khan (1914–44)
Code Name: Madeleine

Largely due to the coverage of her work in the bestselling novel (and the movie made for television) *A Man Called Intrepid*, Noor Inayat Khan may be one of the best-known female operatives of the Second World War. Ironically, she was an incredibly unlikely candidate for the role of undercover agent. Noor was a deeply religious Indian princess and also a confirmed pacifist, who objected to any type of violence. Yet, despite her privileged background and her strong religious beliefs, Noor was committed to the fight against Nazism.

Hazrat Inayat Khan and his American wife Amina Sharada Begum (formerly Ora Ray Baker) welcomed their first child into the world on 1 January 1914. They were living in Moscow when their daughter Noor, which means 'light of womanhood', was born. Khan and his wife had initially travelled to Russia when his musical group, The Royal Musicians of Hindustan, were invited to perform in a Moscow nightclub, and the group became very popular among Moscow's cultural elite. The Khans felt very much at home in Moscow and decided to extend their stay, purchasing a large home not far from the Kremlin. However, Russia was not a stable country in 1914; it was beset with civil unrest and harsh government repression of any individual or groups advocating a freer and more equal society. As the situation in Russia became more uncertain and with the outbreak of the First World War looming, the Khans decided to accept an invitation for their musical group to play an engagement in Paris, where they gave a series of concerts. When war broke out and Germany mobilised against France, the Khans decided to move to Britain with their six-month-old daughter. They stayed for several years, and it was here that Khan formed the Sufi Order. Sufism is a form of Islam, and Hazrat Khan developed an extensive following for his preaching of love, tolerance and pacifism; he published many books on the subject.

Three more children followed Noor – her brothers Hidayat and Vilayat, and sister Khair (later known as Claire) – before the family eventually moved on to France where they settled in Suresnes just outside of Paris. Noor's father was the spiritual leader of the Sufi religious community and his followers supported the Khan family well, allowing them to live a privileged lifestyle. Hazrat Khan travelled to India in the summer of 1926 where he continued his preaching. Sadly, he developed pneumonia during his time there, and died in February 1927 without ever seeing his family again. Noor, her mother and her siblings continued to live in France, still reasonably well supported by Hazrat Khan's followers. At seventeen, Noor enrolled in the École Normale de Musique in Paris where she studied both the piano and harp. She also studied several languages, including French, German and Spanish, and earned a degree in child psychology from the Sorbonne. Upon graduation, Noor embarked on a career as a freelance writer, earning critical acclaim for her children's fairy tales. Khan was not without romance in her life, either. Before his death, Hazrat Khan had planned for Khan to marry an Indian boy, whom Khan met in 1928 and genuinely liked. This marriage was called off a year later, when Khan was fifteen, but she met a young Jewish man during her time at the École Normale de Musique and they eventually became engaged. Her family did not approve of this relationship, but despite their disapproval the pair were engaged for several years. Khan finally called off the engagement just after the Germans attacked France, stating that she 'wanted to be free to go into action or serve as a nurse on the front line if the need arose'.[1]

By 1939, the political situation in Europe had reached its breaking point. Khan was troubled by the violence of the Nazi regime, and Germany's aggression towards its smaller neighbours violated all of her religious principles of peace, tolerance and love. Although she abhorred violence of any kind, Khan was committed to helping stop the Nazi threat and enrolled in a Red Cross nursing course so that she would be able to assist her adopted country in their war effort, should France be attacked. The Germans marched into France in May 1940. The speed of the German advance shocked the British and French troops, and soon had them reeling backwards in retreat towards the English Channel. The German army swept down from the north through Holland and Belgium while launching an armoured assault from the east through the Ardennes Forest in France. In less than a month, the Germans had forced the Allied armies back to the French coast, from where most of the British and some of the French were evacuated back to England. By 10 June, the Germans were approaching the outskirts of

Paris, but Khan and her sister continued their work in the hospital where they were stationed until it was completely evacuated. Khan and her sister then fled south in an attempt to reconnect with their hospital unit. Unable to locate their unit, the pair approached the British consul, who directed them to the port of Saint-Nazaire to join the British Red Cross hospital ship. By the time Khan and her sister reached Saint-Nazaire, however, the hospital ship had sailed. Realising that France was about to fall, Khan and her family made plans to escape to Britain. Since her brother Vilayat had been born in Britain, he managed to secure the family a spot on one of the last boats that had been made available to evacuate British subjects from France.

Khan and her family may have escaped the conquering Germans, but life in Britain presented many challenges. The family settled in Oxford, but in August 1940 the Battle of Britain began, and the Germans seemed closer than ever. Night after night, German bombs rained down on London and its surrounding areas, terrorising civilians. The Khans were also experiencing financial problems. With Germany in control of most of Europe, the Khan family was effectively cut off from the financial support of Hazrat Khan's followers on the Continent. Anxious to continue to be involved in the war effort, and to secure a regular pay cheque for her family, Khan enlisted in the Women's Auxiliary Air Force (WAAF) in November 1940, and was posted to Harrogate as an Aircraftwoman, Second Class. She used the name Nora, as it sounded close to Noor, and listed her religion as Church of England. Her civil occupation was listed as 'writer' and she included 'Fluent French' as one of her other qualifications. Khan was selected for basic training in signals (use of a wireless) and her reports were impressive. Over the next two years Khan was posted to a number of different positions. Much of her time was spent working with various Balloon Barrage groups. Early in 1940 the Royal Air Force (RAF), in an attempt to free up men for active duty elsewhere, had begun using WAAF officers to operate the balloons that floated above British cities and ports. These balloons were used as a defensive measure against German air attack, and were designed to frustrate dive-bombers and to force the German bombers to fly higher so that their bombing was less accurate. Khan was also posted to a bomber command unit where she worked as a radio operator, maintaining communications with British bomber pilots. She rose steadily through the WAAF ranks, and in June 1942 was selected for a more specialised course in signals training. Khan also continued to write during this time, and her fairy tales were often broadcast during the Children's Hour on the BBC.

Khan's fluency in numerous languages, namely French, Spanish and German, had not escaped the attention of her superiors. In October 1942, she received a summons from the War Office to report for an interview with a Captain Selwyn Jepson, who, unbeknown to Khan, was the senior recruiting officer for the Special Operations Executive (SOE). On 10 November 1942, Khan met with Jepson at the Hotel Victoria. Jepson explained to Khan about the need for wireless operators in France and how important it was for the British government to be in contact with the French Resistance. Communications with operatives in France provided the Allies with information about German troop movements and locations of possible bombing targets, and facilitated the rescue of downed Allied airmen. Jepson was also very clear in telling Khan exactly what the consequences of being captured by the Germans entailed. Imprisonment, torture and execution were all to be expected should an agent fall into enemy hands. Khan had misgivings. She indicated that, while working as a wireless operator was exactly the type of assignment she would be willing to take on, she feared her mother would be devastated if she left for overseas work. However, after mulling it over for several days and speaking with her mother, Khan sent a letter to Captain Jepson. It explained that any reservations Khan may have had about leaving her mother had been resolved, and that she realised 'how petty our family ties are when something in the way of winning this war is at stake'.[2] Before accepting Khan for training, Jepson, as with all candidates, asked her where her loyalties lay. Khan was her usual truthful self, stating that her first loyalty was to India, and if she had to choose between Britain or India, then India would win out. Slightly taken aback, Jepson countered by explaining that, at the moment, Khan merely had to choose what she felt about the Germans. Khan declared she loathed the Germans and wanted to see them lose the war. Jepson immediately accepted her as an SOE candidate, and she was sent home to Abingdon to await orders.

Early in February of 1943, Khan was sent to Wanborough Manor to begin her SOE training. Wanborough was a beautiful estate in Surrey and was the first school that 'F' Section agents would attend during the course of their training. Many SOE candidates were weeded out during this time but Khan successfully completed the four-week course, which consisted of basic military and physical training. It was at Wanborough that Khan met fellow agents Yolande Beekman and Cecily Lefort, two women who would ultimately share her tragic fate. Khan's instructors noted that she was rather clumsy, which hampered her performance in such areas as physical training, fieldcraft, and explosives and demolitions, but she performed very well in signalling, having already completed two courses of signals training. Her instructor's remarks read, 'Lacked confidence to begin with but has come on very well and shows considerable promise. Active, plenty of spirit, and could be relied upon to come up to scratch when the occasion arose.'[3]

From Wanborough, Khan moved on to Thame Park, where she received more intensive training in coding and ciphering. She understood coding theory very well, and received satisfactory reports on her accuracy and efficiency in sending and receiving transmissions. Khan laboured for hours each day, increasing her Morse speed and learning how to diagnose and repair problems with a wireless set, as well as how to hide the set and set up aerials. Having already had a good deal of radio-transmission training she was ahead of all of the other trainees. She also developed a deeper understanding of exactly how dangerous it would be to be sent on a mission as a wireless operator. The radio set was very heavy and would have to be carried from place to place in order to vary transmission sites. It could be taken apart but each section looked distinctly like a piece of radio equipment, so even disassembled it would be difficult to explain the possession of such a piece to the Germans. The sets also produced a very weak signal and required a huge antenna (about 21 m), which was not only troublesome to erect but also difficult to hide. Operators were made very aware that German radio detection equipment was superior to the British technology. In practice the candidate agents had about an hour to elude the British radio locators; however, in Occupied France they would have about half that amount of time. It is interesting that there were two stages of training that Khan was not required to complete. Unlike most other agents, she received no parachute training, as her instructors had declared her unsuitable for jumping (although no specific reason was given). There is also no evidence that Khan ever completed training at Arisaig (where agents were trained in the art of guerilla warfare tactics). This would have been a typical progression for most agents after their Wanborough stint, but it would be reasonable to assume that SOE was more interested in having Khan refine her wireless-operation skills than in teaching her how to blow things up.

Khan did not fare as well at the next level of her training. At Beaulieu she was to complete her security course. Agents were taught various types of clandestine techniques and security measures. Skills such as spotting someone following you, knowing when to change your address and altering your personality were drilled into prospective agents. Khan's dreamy and truthful nature made her thoughtless about security, and she had extreme difficulty concealing her real personality. One of her instructors, Lieutenant Holland, reported that Khan had indicated 'she would not like to do anything two-faced ... deliberately cultivating friendly relations with malice aforethought'.[4] Instructors were concerned about her shattered reaction to the mock German interrogation they put her through. Her escorting officer, Joan Sanderson, found Khan's reaction to her mock interrogation almost unbearable. She seemed absolutely terrified. One saw that the lights hurt her, and the officer's voice when he shouted very loudly. Once he said, 'Stand on that chair!' It was just something to confuse her. She was so overwhelmed, nearly lost her voice. As it went on she became practically inaudible. Sometimes there was only a whisper. When she came out afterwards, she was trembling and quite blanched.[5]

Even fellow agents questioned her suitability for field work, wondering whether this daydreamer, who was heavily immersed in astrology and palm-reading, had the temperament to fulfill such a high-pressure role as an undercover operative. Yvonne Cormeau, an SOE agent who trained with Khan and survived the war, stated that Khan was a 'splendid, dreamy creature, far too conspicuous – twice seen, never forgotten who had no sense of security and should never have been sent into France'.[6] Two other female agents approached Vera Atkins, assistant to Maurice Buckmaster (head of 'F' Section), with their own concerns about Khan's suitability. Atkins met with Khan to convey the concerns that had been expressed, and gave Khan the opportunity to leave SOE. Khan was hurt by her colleagues' doubts, and refused Atkins' offer.[7]

One of Khan's final security training exercises was a ninety-six-hour scheme; she was sent to Bristol in order to establish a fake identity, recruit people to work with, set up message drops and find a safe place from which to send radio transmissions. SOE instructors observed her at all times to determine her security consciousness. Khan performed well for most of the scheme with the exception of the interrogation. Her instructor reported that Khan had been quite diligent and had 'shown interest in the exercise, but however, must learn to be more discreet. Apart from the police interrogation, I consider this quite a good scheme.'[8] Khan's personnel file is littered with reports that cast doubts upon her suitability for clandestine work. Her final report, written by Colonel Frank Spooner on 21 May 1943, was perhaps the bluntest, stating, 'Not overburdened with brains but has worked hard and shown keenness, apart from some dislike of the security side of the course. She has an unstable and temperamental personality and it is very doubtful whether she is really suited to work in the field.'[9]

Maurice Buckmaster chose to disregard Spooner's concerns, and his notes such as 'Nonsense' and 'Makes me cross' can be found scribbled in the margins of Spooner's final report on Khan. It was not unusual for Buckmaster to overrule his instructors' opinions regarding agent suitability, as he did the same with agents Violette Szabo and Odette Sansom. In fact, in his book, *Specially Employed*, he explained some of the reasons for an agent being sent into the field despite having less than stellar training reports. He stated, 'It was necessary, for overriding reasons of shortage of specialists – particularly wireless operators – to stretch a point in favour of the candidate.'[10] It was an undeniable fact that, in the summer of 1943, wireless operators were desperately needed in Occupied France. Message traffic from the Paris area was overwhelming and, although she had not yet completed her security training, Khan was SOE's best-prepared wireless operator. A note in her file reveals, 'This student was withdrawn … at the request of her Country Section. While she cannot be considered a fully

so that they would be able to join the fight when the Allies invaded the Continent. Cinema introduced Khan to the PROSPER team, which included Suttill, wireless operator Gilbert Norman, and courier Andrée Borrel. They had no idea how little time they would have to work together.

Khan's lack of security awareness became obvious immediately. The day after her arrival in Paris, Khan was taken to PROSPER's working headquarters, which was located at an agricultural school at Grignon, just north-west of Versailles. Members of PROSPER were shocked when Khan casually left the briefcase containing all of her codes on the front table in the entrance hall of the school. She was also reprimanded for pouring milk into her teacup, before adding the tea. This distinctly English mannerism would easily catch the attention of any sharp-eyed German. However, PROSPER agents soon had bigger things to worry about than their new wireless operator's absent-mindedness. The circuit had been betrayed by a double agent, and large-scale arrests were decimating the network's numbers. Francis Suttill, Gilbert Norman and Andrée Borrel were all arrested just a week after Khan arrived in France, and the PROSPER network began to disintegrate. Wave after wave of arrests took place, the group's headquarters at Grignon was raided and Khan herself reported back to London that all of PROSPER's leaders and equipment had been captured. SOE immediately ordered Khan back to Britain. She refused, claiming that, as one of the few wireless operators still in operation, SOE could little afford to lose her transmissions. Khan began life on the run, travelling from place to place around Paris and its outskirts, trying to find safe areas from which to transmit. By the end of June, Khan's radio was the only one that 'F' Section had in the Paris region that was still operational.

Khan continued to roam the surrounding areas of Paris, looking up old friends and staying one step ahead of the Gestapo. She actively sought out safe houses to transmit from, preferring houses with gardens, or flats with trees adjacent, so that she would have some place to hang her aerial. Occasionally friends who had cars would drive her out into the country so that she could transmit outside the city. SOE once again gave her the opportunity of returning to Britain, but Khan felt that she could re-establish some of the broken Resistance networks and that her transmissions were more important than ever. SOE warned her only to receive messages (received messages could not be tracked) and not to transmit, since all German direction-finding devices would be trained on her radio. Khan ignored these warnings, and began regular transmissions to London starting the first week of July. Her transmissions focused mainly on providing updates on the status of the network, and on identifying locations for drops of arms, ammunition and money, which would be picked up by members of the French Resistance. On one occasion, desperate for a place to transmit from, Khan returned to Grignon, her original transmission site. She was dismayed to find the agricultural school occupied by the Germans, and had to make a quick escape under heavy fire. Her citation for the French Croix de Guerre states, 'Falling into an ambush at GRIGNON, in July 1943, her comrades and she managed to escape after having killed or wounded the Germans who tried to stop them.' There is also evidence that Khan was involved in providing assistance to Allied airmen who had been shot down over France. While information regarding the extent of her assistance has not been preserved, there is a commendation in her personnel file that states, 'She was instrumental in facilitating the escape of 30 Allied airmen shot down in FRANCE.'[13] Most likely her involvement was linked to her role as a wireless operator, and perhaps she provided the communication link, with either London or other SOE networks, that enabled these airmen to escape from Occupied France.

Khan was optimistic that the war would soon be over, and events taking place in Europe seemed to support this hope. General Montgomery had defeated General Rommel in North Africa, Allied troops had landed in Sicily and the Russians were attacking German positions along the Eastern Front. Khan felt that the information she was sending from Paris would prove invaluable to the Allied armies in their preparation for an invasion of the Continent. An excerpt from one of her postcards to SOE reveals her cheerful state: 'Thanks a lot! It's grand working [with] you. The best moments I have had yet.'[14] She changed her hair colour to disguise her appearance, purchased a bicycle so that she could remain mobile, and continued her transmissions to London.

All through the summer Khan managed to stay one step ahead of the Gestapo. However, German counter-intelligence was operating in full force in Paris, and German soldiers filled the streets. Khan had several narrow escapes. One such incident occurred on the metro, when two German officers became suspicious of the suitcase Khan was carrying. The suitcase, of course, contained her radio, which she was forced to carry with her now that she was constantly on the move. However, she breezily told the two officers that the suitcase contained a cinematograph projector and even opened the case to show them what she was carrying! Thankfully, the officers did not recognise the contraption as a wireless transmitter. Khan's nerve, which instructors at Beaulieu had questioned, was now serving her very well. She managed to elude the Germans for months, transmitting when she could and compiling a list of all of the agents who had survived the PROSPER arrests. However, the net around Khan was slowly closing in. German counter-intelligence officers were picking off her contacts one by one, and it became increasingly dangerous to meet with any of her fellow agents, as Khan could never be sure who might have been captured and forced to work for the Germans. In late September 1943, Khan had a meeting scheduled with another agent. The agent never showed up and Khan feared that he had been arrested. She shared her worries with a friend who worked in the Resistance, and together they decided to call the agent's apartment to discover what had happened to him. The agent answered his phone, and tried to convince Khan to come to his apartment. Khan was suspicious, since she had never been to his apartment before, and insisted they meet in a more public place, on the corner of the Avenue Mac-Mahon and the Rue de Tilsitt. The agent agreed. Khan waited at the Arc de Triomphe where she had a full view of the meeting place. Her friend drove up and down the Avenue Mac-Mahon, observing the agent seated on a bench with several suspicious-looking men posted along the length of the block. After waiting approximately forty minutes, the agent and the suspicious-looking men all got into a car and left the meeting place together. Clearly,

Khan had avoided an ambush that the agent, under German control, had attempted to set up.

As a wireless operator, Khan's biggest threat was from German radio-direction-finding devices. The Germans had identified her signal but Khan's constant movements made her impossible to pin down. She would transmit briefly and then immediately travel to a new location. In an extract from an official statement, the Commandant of the Paris Gestapo, Hans Kieffer, noted, 'I remember the English W/T operator, Madeleine ... We were pursuing her for months and as we had a personal description of her we arranged for all stations to be watched. She had several addresses and worked very carefully.'[15] German direction-finding technology, however, would not prove her undoing. Rather, in early autumn of 1943, Khan was betrayed when a woman contacted the Gestapo with an offer to 'sell' them Madeleine. The Gestapo was familiar with Khan's code name and knew exactly how important the information that the woman was offering to sell them was. They purchased Khan's address from the woman and, during the second week of October, Khan returned to her apartment to find a Gestapo officer waiting for her. Khan struggled with the officer, scratching and biting and putting up such resistance that he had to call in other officers to assist in bringing her in. The Gestapo confiscated her radio transmitter and a school copybook that she always carried with her, which contained all of her messages and security checks. Khan's notebook violated SOE security instructions, which clearly stated that all codes needed to be committed to memory and never written down for someone to find. However, in her assignment instructions, it clearly states, 'Be very careful in the filing of your messages.'[16] It is believed that Khan simply misunderstood the meaning of the word filing: to file one's messages meant to send or transmit; Khan obviously thought it meant to keep careful record of her transmissions. Because of this misunderstanding, all of Khan's messages were carefully documented in her notebook. The notebook, in German hands, was to have tragic results.

Khan was taken to German counter-intelligence headquarters at the infamous Avenue Foch, where she was initially interrogated by Ernst Vogt. She attempted escape less than an hour after being brought in. Demanding to be allowed to bathe, Khan threw a tantrum when she realised the guards were planning on keeping the door to the bathroom open. She made such a fuss that Vogt agreed to allow the door to be shut. Khan wasted no time, and quickly climbed out of the bathroom window. She was spotted on the ledge by Vogt, however, and he very quietly, so as not to startle her and cause her to fall, leaned out of the window and said, 'Madeleine, don't be silly. You will kill yourself. Think of your mother! Give me your hand!'[17] Over the next five weeks, she was interrogated almost daily. The Germans urged her to play back her radio for them, but Khan was steadfast in her refusal. Hans Kieffer stated, 'Madeleine, after her capture, showed great courage and we got no information whatsoever out of her.'[18] Ultimately, the Germans did not need Khan to operate her radio for them. With her codebook in hand, the Germans were able to continue transmitting to London using Khan's security checks. It wasn't until early 1944 that SOE realised that Khan had been captured, and by that time the Germans' use of Khan's radio had had several tragic results, including the capture of several SOE agents who had been dropped into France at location spots transmitted by Khan's radio. All of those agents were later executed.

Khan made a second escape attempt from Avenue Foch with two other male prisoners. She had made contact with a Frenchman, Colonel Leon Faye, by tapping out Morse code messages to him between their cells. The other man was Captain John Starr. Starr had been arrested by the Germans in July and, in an effort to save his own life, had shown himself willing to work with them. Starr knew Khan was at Avenue Foch and managed to slip a note under her door one evening. They arranged to keep up correspondence by leaving messages under the basin in the lavatory. The three devised a plan to escape, using a stolen screwdriver to loosen the bars on the skylights in the ceilings of their rooms. On the night of 25 November 1943, the three prisoners managed to remove the skylight bars and make their way onto the roof of 84 Avenue Foch. With their shoes hanging around their necks and their blankets (to be tied together to make a rope for their descent) in their hands, they made their way across the rooftops of the surrounding buildings. Suddenly, air-raid sirens went off. Anti-aircraft fire exploded around them and searchlights lit up the rooftops in response to an RAF attack. The three knew their escape would soon be discovered, as the cells were always checked during an air raid. As they attempted to climb down to the next roof, they saw the block was surrounded by Germans. The trio tried to take refuge in one of the buildings, but were soon apprehended and returned to Avenue Foch. The officer in charge demanded that Khan promise to make no more escape attempts. She was steadfast in her refusal (unlike Starr who was more than happy to comply) and was immediately sent to a German civil prison in Pforzheim. Labelled as a dangerous prisoner because of her lack of cooperation and her escape attempts, Khan was kept in chains throughout her incarceration. In a sworn statement, the Governor of Pforzheim prison, Wilhelm Krauss, explained, 'I was told that she was to be treated in accordance with regulations for Nacht und Nebel prisoners [note: Nacht und Nebel means Night and Fog. It was the expression used for people who disappeared and, once in custody, were kept on the lowest rations, in solitary confinement, etc.] and moreover that she was to be chained hand and foot.'[19] It was a degrading situation as she was unable to bathe or feed herself. For almost ten months she remained chained and in solitary confinement. A fellow prisoner at Pforzheim, Yolande Lagrave, befriended Khan and they, along with two other French girls, began to communicate by scratching messages on their food bowls. Lagrave recalled that Khan used the name Nora Baker (another one of her aliases) and that she was 'very unhappy. Hands and feet were manacled, she was never taken out and I could hear that she was beaten up.'[20] Khan's messages would often ask the girls to think of her, as she was so unhappy, or for any updates they might have as to how the war was going. Her final message, scratched onto her bowl in September 1944, read simply, 'I am leaving.'[21]

On 11 September 1944, the Gestapo removed Khan from Pforzheim prison. Along with three other female prisoners – Yolande Beekman, Eliane Plewman and Madeleine Damerment – who had been collected from nearby Karlsruhe prison, Khan travelled by train to her next, and final, destination. They were told they were destined for a camp where they would do agricultural work, but, in fact, the order for their execution had already been given. The train ride was leisurely, and the women enjoyed the picturesque mountain scenery, and the chance to talk among themselves and smoke some English cigarettes. The train arrived at Dachau concentration camp, located in southern Germany, around midnight. Dachau was one of the most infamous of all Nazi concentration camps. Built in 1933, it was designated as an extermination camp in 1941, and throughout the war countless executions took place within its fences. What exactly happened on the morning of 13 September 1944 is the subject of some controversy. The official report, found in Khan's personnel file, indicates that the women were given separate cells and then early the next morning all four were brought to a sandy spot in the camp yard. As the orders for their executions were read out, the women knelt in the sand, side by side. A bullet was put through the back of each woman's neck and their bodies were quickly dispatched to the crematorium. However, there are several other accounts from individuals who were at Dachau, which say that Khan was 'centred out' for special treatment; they state that she was beaten and tortured the entire night of 12/13 September 1944 and was actually shot in her cell.

Khan's fate was initially unknown to SOE. After the war, Vera Atkins travelled to Europe attempting to track down what exactly had happened to the agents who had not returned. She originally thought, due to mistaken eyewitness accounts, that Khan had been one of the four women executed (and allegedly burned alive) at the Natzweiler camp on 6 July 1944. These women were Andrée Borrel, Vera

Leigh, Diana Rowden and a woman who was described as being very petite with dark hair. From the descriptions given by individuals who had been at Natzweiler, including SOE agent Brian Stonehouse, Atkins was convinced that the fourth girl was Khan. A formal death notification was sent by the War Office to Khan's family, and her brother Vilayat remembers receiving the notification, telling a family friend, 'I've found out what happened to my sister. She was burned alive...'[22] Khan's mother was already devastated by the loss of her daughter, and Khan's siblings kept the details of the death notification from her. Khan's brother asked that all communication from the War Office be done through him, to spare his mother the anguish. Vilayat continued to search for details of his sister's death, and soon became confused about the conflicting information he was receiving. He received a letter from Yolande Legrave, who said she had been incarcerated with Khan at Pforzheim prison and that Khan had left the prison for an unknown destination in September 1944. This meant that Khan was alive after her supposed 6 July 1944 execution. Khan's brother pressed the War Office to look into these discrepancies, and Vera Atkins resumed her investigation. Poring over Pforzheim records, Atkins discovered that Khan had been at Pforzheim and had been transferred to Dachau in September 1944. Atkins confirmed that Khan was executed the morning after her arrival, and later established the identity of the petite, brown-haired woman who was executed at Natzweiler as Sonia Olschanezky, a courier for the JUGGLER circuit. Three years after Khan's death, her true fate was finally known.

Noor Inayat Khan received numerous medals for her

bravery, including the George Cross (Britain's highest civilian honour), Member of the British Empire and the French Croix de Guerre with gold star (France's highest civilian award). The role she played as the sole link of communication with Paris was considered to be the most important and dangerous posting in France during the summer of 1943. She refused to abandon her post and ultimately paid with her life. Khan's bravery and sacrifice have not been forgotten. Her name can be found on numerous memorial plaques: at Dachau, St Paul's church (London), the RAF Memorial in Runnymede, and on the Memorial Gates to the Commonwealth Soldiers in Hyde Park. There is a small plaque bearing her name that can be found at the agricultural college in Grignon where she made her first transmissions, and a plaque outside her childhood home in Suresnes reads,

Here lived Noor Inayat Khan 1914–44
Called Madeleine in the Resistance
Shot at Dachau
Radio Operator for the Buckmaster network.[23]

Sonia Butt (1924–2014)
Code Name: Blanche/Madeleine

Many of the Special Operations Executive's best undercover agents during the Second World War were Canadians. Frank Pickersgill, John 'Ken' Macalister, Gustave Bieler and Guy d'Artois, as well as numerous other Canadian men, served bravely as agents in enemy-occupied territory; some, including Pickersgill, Macalister and Bieler, paid with their lives. However, Canada's only claim to a female undercover agent comes through marriage. War bride Sonia Butt came to Canada in 1946 with her husband, fellow SOE agent Guy d'Artois. She brought with her a fascinating story about her exploits as one of the youngest female SOE operatives ever sent into Occupied France.

Sonia (who changed the spelling of her name to Sonya in her twenties) was a beautiful girl and the daughter of a Royal Air Force (RAF) group captain Leslie Butt and his wife Thelma Gordon. She was born at Eastchurch, Kent, on 14 May 1924, and her parents separated when Sonia was two years old. She spent much of her childhood in France, being educated in private schools while her father was working in North Africa. Sixteen-year-old Sonia was in the middle of her school term when Germany launched its attack against France, sending its tanks tearing through the Ardennes

Forest. Alone, as her mother was visiting Britain, and without a passport (it was common during this time for children to be registered on their parents' passport), Sonia found herself in an extremely difficult situation. Without proper identification or a passport, leaving France and entering Britain seemed almost impossible. With the German advance showing no sign of slowing down, Sonia decided she needed to take action to protect herself. Demonstrating incredible nerve, Sonia borrowed the money for her travelling expenses from her headmistress, and travelled, on her own, to Calais, where British refugees were departing for Britain. Using all of her charm she managed to talk her way past the French emigration authorities and managed to get aboard one of the last passenger ships that was able to depart for Britain. Alone, Sonia made the dangerous voyage across the English Channel and pleaded with British immigration authorities to let her into the country. With no one at the port to meet her, Sonia borrowed some more money, this time from a family friend, and was eventually able to board a train which allowed her to reunite with her mother. Obviously, even at the tender age of sixteen, Sonia was an extremely resourceful young woman. Unfortunately, being reunited with her family did not mean that Sonia had escaped the German danger. After her arrival, she experienced first-hand the horrors of war. The Battle of Britain raged over British skies for almost a year as the German Luftwaffe attempted to bomb the British into submission. Originally the bombing raids focused on airfields, factories and naval yards but, when this failed to make a dent in British resolve, the Germans soon started selecting civilian targets. Hundreds of RAF pilots lost their lives defending the skies over Britain, and Sonia, as a civilian, feared not only for her own safety but also for that of her father.

Sonia spent the next couple of years focused on her studies and trying to live life as a normal teenager under wartime conditions. By eighteen Sonia had completed her schooling (including getting her diploma from what she called a 'domestic school') and decided to take an active part in the war effort. She joined the Women's Auxiliary Air Force (WAAF) and was assigned administrative duties at RAF Gosforth. This proved rather tiresome for the active and adventurous young girl, who quite often found herself at the centre of some sort of mischief. As punishment for her occasional high jinks, Sonia found herself spending a great deal of time on kitchen duty, usually peeling potatoes, and both she and her good friend Paddy O'Sullivan felt that their talents were being wasted. O'Sullivan thought that working as a translator might be more challenging and she applied for a position. Paddy's interview was conducted by a Special Operations Executive recruiter, and once she discovered what the job entailed she urged Sonia to apply as well. Paddy was not able to reveal to Butt the true nature of the posting, so Sonia was quite surprised when she arrived for her interview at a luxurious Oxford Sreet apartment. Her surprise quickly turned to excitement, however, when she discovered that she was being considered for work as a secret agent. Sonia seemed to make an excellent impression upon all who met her, and she so impressed the SOE recruiters that they immediately recommended her for training school, despite her young age. After her command of the French language was thoroughly examined and she had been transferred from the WAAF to the First Aid Nursing Yeomanry (FANY),

Butt was sent on a training course at Wanborough Manor. She found herself housed with a group of fellow agents, most of whom had French-speaking backgrounds; there were French Canadians, British men and women who had been educated in France, French-speaking citizens from the British colony of Mauritius, and South Africans who had lived in the French colony of Madagascar. Along with fellow SOE recruit Nancy Wake and her friend Paddy O'Sullivan (who was eventually sent to France as a wireless operator), she was put through a variety of tests designed to assess her personality and her eye for detail. Butt, ever the good sport, obligingly completed all of the tests, proving to be a resourceful and self-reliant young lady.

The instructors watched the recruits carefully for behavioural 'slips' that might compromise their security in France. All conversations at meals were expected to be in French, and those who made too many mistakes were removed from the course. Butt experienced first-hand what lengths the instructors would go to in order to determine an agent's ability to maintain his or her cover. One evening, after a session of heavy drinking (which was encouraged by the school authorities in order to help them evaluate an agent's propensity for loose lips), she awoke to find an instructor sitting by her bed to see what language she spoke if she talked in her sleep! Candidates were put through exercises where they had to evaluate a stranger's character so they would be better prepared to spot enemy agents and to select trustworthy people to work with in the field. They were also expected to learn how to steal, both from other students' quarters and from locked and guarded rooms. The candidate agents did not only need to be able to enter mix materials to create explosive devices, practising by demolishing small bits of railway track and some unfortunate trees. From there it was on to finishing school at the Beaulieu estate in the New Forest, where candidates were instructed on how to maintain their personal security. They were trained to detect if they were being followed and in how to blend in with crowds, and were also put through mock interrogations that gave them an idea of what to expect if they were captured. All recruits were given specific instructions that if they were arrested they needed to withstand torture for at least forty-eight hours to provide enough time for the other agents that they were working with to get away. A final training exercise, in Manchester, required Butt to rent a room and establish her identity as a young widow with a small child. Butt used a photo of her younger brother to depict her 'son'. As part of the exercise, she returned to her room one evening and found that it had been ransacked; she was subsequently arrested and interrogated by instructors who were posing as Gestapo officers. Butt performed well during her mock interrogation, but generally her instructors were worried about her young age. Some felt that she lacked the maturity to fill the role of an SOE operative. However, Maurice Buckmaster, who was in charge of SOE's French Section ('F' Section), spoke to her, basically advising that she stop acting so much like a teenager. It was tough advice for the high-spirited young woman, but she took it to heart since she was determined to succeed. Following Buckmaster's advice Butt became much more serious and focused, and went on to complete her parachute training at Ringway with Guy d'Artois. Butt and d'Artois had continued to become closer, and now that and with the invasion of Europe (D-Day) fast approaching, Buckmaster granted her wish. D'Artois was assigned to the DITCHER network and was parachuted into the Burgundy region of France on 1 May 1944. Butt, who had no idea where her husband had been sent, was herself parachuted into France near Le Mans nine days before D-Day. Late one evening, almost a month after she had watched her husband depart for his mission, Butt was transferred to RAF Tempsford where she met with Buckmaster, who had come down to say goodbye, and to give her a cigarette case and compact as a going-away present. He also gave her a final briefing on her assignment. Butt would be parachuting into France with both a wireless operator and a demolitions specialist. Her job, specifically, was to recruit, arm and train French Resistance members so that they could effectively sabotage and harass the German forces occupying the region. Butt was also instructed to gather as much information as possible about German strength and troop movements in the area so that it might be transmitted, via wireless, back to Britain. After reviewing her instructions, Buckmaster handed Butt an envelope containing several small white tablets, and a more ominous single blue capsule. The white, he explained, were stimulants that she was to use if she ever required extra endurance to complete a mission. The single blue capsule was to be used if she was ever captured and found herself suffering, beyond what she could stand, at the hands of German interrogators. Slipping the envelope into her pocket, the single blue capsule served as a chilling reminder to Butt of the danger she was about to face.

Butt's cover story, which gave her the alias Suzanne Bonvie, was meticulously researched and designed to provide her with a background that was both believable and difficult to trace. Her 'fake' home town was a place that had been bombed flat by the Allies, so that both the town records and the house itself were destroyed. Her cover story was that she was a representative for a Paris design house and was travelling to Le Mans to stay with a cousin, Jean-Paul Bonvie, who had a home there, in order to recover from a bout of bronchitis. The last name, Bonvie, actually did belong to a man who owned a home just outside of Le Mans, and that man was a member of the French Resistance. A lovely designer wardrobe was procured for Butt to support her identity as someone who worked in the fashion industry. As pretty things and new clothes were difficult to come by in wartime Britain, Butt was over the moon with this aspect of her story! She was given the code names Blanche and Madeleine, and was assigned to the HEADMASTER network.

Sydney Hudson, HEADMASTER organiser, had been given the task of building up a network of Resistance groups to harass the German army in coordination with the D-Day invasion. While Hudson didn't know the actual date of D-Day (a well-kept secret), he knew it was imminent, and that he needed to train, equip and deploy the Resistance groups in a timely manner. To do this effectively, he needed a courier, and he knew that a female would have much more freedom to move around the countryside than a male. He sent his request for a female courier in the middle of May 1944 and, on the 28th, Butt, along with Raimond Glaesner, Eugene Bec and several containers of weapons and explosives, was dropped into Hudson's sector. Butt was terrified as she looked out over the landing zone;

through fear, adrenaline, or just bad luck, she bungled her jump despite having completed four perfect practice jumps. Unable to fight the urge to look down, Butt forgot her trainer's instructions to keep her head up as she exited the hatch or risk flipping over and twisting the shroud lines. Her lines twisted and she struggled to right herself during her descent. Dressed in a skirt, sweater, overalls (to keep her warm in the unheated plane) and ski boots, which were designed to protect her feet and ankles on landing, Butt hit the ground hard, crashing down in the middle of a ditch and injuring her shoulder.

Stunned and shaken after her jarring impact, she struggled to make sense of her surroundings. She heard a rumbling noise in the distance and, certain that anything making that much noise must be the enemy, decided she needed to quickly release and bury her parachute. Unfortunately, her lines had been fouled during her awkward descent, and she was hopelessly entrapped. Dragging her parachute behind her with her pistol in her hand, she slowly made her way across a field to a grove of trees, which would at least provide some cover. Butt could still hear the rumbling noise in the distance, and correctly assumed it was some kind of convoy. Suddenly a group of men appeared through the trees, and Butt gripped her pistol more tightly, anticipating a firefight. A French voice whispered, 'It is a woman.'[3] Butt relaxed as a group of elderly Frenchmen gathered around her. They explained to her that the man who was supposed to meet her had been killed by the Germans a few days earlier. The detachment in the way the men spoke about death chilled Butt, and she was hit with the realisation that, for the French living under German occupation, violent

Butt's 'drop' was considered a success, with one minor exception. The container carrying her wardrobe was not recovered by the reception committee and Butt was incensed when it was picked up by a German patrol. This container of women's clothing gave the Germans a clue that there was a new female agent working in the area, but Butt refused to 'lay low', and began work immediately. Her new commanding officer, Sydney Hudson, was impressed with his new courier, not only because of her work ethic, but also because of her beauty. He remembers thinking that she was 'an extremely pretty girl'.[7] Butt and Hudson had met earlier in London, and they had developed feelings for one another, but he was married and Butt was involved with Guy d'Artois. When they discovered they had been teamed together on this mission, both Butt and Hudson knew that an emotional entanglement was going to be difficult to avoid. Butt recalled that her first thought upon seeing Hudson was, 'My God. How am I going to handle this?'[8]

Butt spent her first several days in France at the Château Le Breuil St Michel, where she became very close to the owner, Madame de Sevenet. De Sevenet's son was a member of the Resistance, and had recently been killed in a friendly fire incident. Butt was introduced as a relative of the de Sevenets in order to explain her presence to the many German officers who were occupying the chateau, and she mixed freely and convincingly in her new surroundings. She even took the opportunity to make use of the chateau's chapel, where she was baptised (Sonia was Anglican, but had promised to convert to her husband Guy's Catholic faith). New clothes were an immediate necessity, since hers had been lost in the drop and the ones she was wearing were too hot for the mild

June temperatures. Hudson had a contact who ran a small clothing store, and Butt was duly outfitted. She was pleased to discover that her SOE training made it quite easy for her to pass as a French civilian. In training she had studied how to use the Occupation ration books, and she made several purchases with ease. This was a great relief to her, as the Germans often altered rationing regulations in order to 'make it difficult for underground organisers to slip quietly into the life of a French community'.[9] She also acquired a bike, and knew exactly how much it cost and where to apply for a licence. Butt proved to her new co-workers early on that she was not some shrinking violet. Hudson recalled how, during an Allied bombing raid (actually the start of D-Day) on a nearby railway station, he had rushed upstairs to comfort Butt and soothe her fears. There was no need, since Butt was completely unfazed by the explosions. Her strength of nerve failed her, however, when it came to threats of a reptilian nature. On one of her first nights in France she was given a tent of her own for accommodation. When she awoke to discover a snake under her sleeping bag, she screamed bloody murder; from that point on, she shared a tent with the men.

With the date of D-Day still unknown, but driven by the knowledge that it could happen at any time, Butt and Hudson began working around the clock. Sonia was responsible for numerous tasks, including scouting for suitable drop zones and looking for safe houses for radio transmissions. Daily broadcasts from the British Broadcasting Company (BBC) carried messages to agents, often in the form of ridiculous sentences, such as 'the canary has laid an egg'. While these sentences appeared nonsensical, and the British made no effort to disguise them in their broadcasts, the agents who were listening in would have been prepped to know exactly what the messages meant. It was in this manner, over the BBC, that orders were received instructing SOE agents and Resistance teams to attack or sabotage roads, telephone lines and rail transportation. Butt's expertise with explosives was in high demand, as the Resistance workers needed instruction so that they could complete their sabotage work. She also cycled hundreds of miles acting as Hudson's courier, coordinating the actions of all the Resistance groups in the Le Mans region. In an effort to raise the numbers in their group, Butt appealed to an influential Le Mans priest, Father LeBlanc. It was a difficult conversation, as neither Butt nor the priest was willing to trust the other. Butt was too security conscious to simply blurt out that she was with the Resistance and that they needed him to help them recruit more men! Father LeBlanc, too, was cautious, as he had no way to be sure Butt was not a German spy. Finally, deciding to take a risk, Butt asked Father LeBlanc to select any phrase he wanted, and to listen to the French news broadcast over the BBC the next evening. The priest chose the phrase 'the meek shall inherit the earth'.[10] Butt had the group's radio operator send an urgent message to London: 'Imperative BBC broadcast tomorrow night on French service 7.30 p.m. the following words...'[11] Father LeBlanc's chosen phrase was broadcast the following evening, and the priest became one of the group's biggest allies, urging his parishioners to join the fight. The HEADMASTER circuit had become a force to be reckoned with. Butt and Hudson made an effective team professionally, and on a more personal level their mutual attraction continued to grow.

Butt was extremely busy in the days leading up to D-Day. Hudson put her in charge of the group's finances, which were used to purchase civilian goods, pay rent on safe houses, and bribe officials and civilians alike. Butt and Hudson also decided to mix blatantly with the Germans, gambling that they would be far less suspicious if they appeared to thrive on German company. They often dined at black market restaurants that were frequented by German officers. According to Butt, she mixed so well with the Germans that

> many French who didn't know me scowled at me ... I was taken for an 'officer girl'. Because of my fair hair some of the French thought I was German. There were German officers who suspected I was in their own secret service. I left them to puzzle. It all helped to confuse the issue.[12]

Butt had been told by Buckmaster that one of the reasons she was chosen as an agent was that she was a very attractive woman.[13] She recognised how useful her beauty could be and made a concerted effort to establish 'friendly' relations with the Germans. Butt's willingness to chat and flirt with the German officers made her privy to information that she was quick to relay over the wireless to London. One officer in particular, a German colonel, showed serious interest in Butt, and she was quite sure that he wanted to pursue a deeper relationship. One evening, as the two sat chatting in a café, Butt's handbag, which held her revolver, slipped off the back of her chair and made a loud, metallic clunk as it hit the floor. From the Colonel's penetrating gaze, Butt got the sense that he knew exactly what was in her purse, and, thinking fast, she reached into her purse and pulled out a forged firearms permit that had been signed by the Gestapo. Butt recalled,

> From that moment the colonel and I understood each other. I was a Gestapo spy, probably the mistress of a high Gestapo officer, which accounted to him for a lot of things – why I frequented the expensive black-market cafes, why I never let him accompany me to my quarters. I was a dangerous person but that lent spice to our tête-à-têtes. He was playing with fire, he let me know in so many words – but he liked it.[14]

She had another near miss a short while after. As Butt was heading for a meeting at a safe house, she recalled developing a strange premonition that something was wrong. 'Something compelled me to turn back. At the bottom of the street I passed a man I knew. Without looking at me he said, "It's blown."'[15]

Her instincts saved her life, as an informer had advised the Germans that a new female agent would be arriving at the home. The Gestapo was waiting for her at the safe house, but she never arrived. Ironically, Butt's German colonel had shared with her that the Germans were well aware that a new female agent had been parachuted in and was working in the area, noting that they expected to arrest the woman very soon. Butt simply shuddered and told him she could never imagine herself having the courage to jump out of a plane, secretly amused that the colonel had no idea how close to that new female agent he was!

On the morning of D-Day, 6 June 1944, Butt was dining in a café when she heard the official radio broadcast that the invasion had begun. Radio instructions to the HEADMASTER circuit had contained orders for Resistance groups to disrupt German communications by attacking railways, roads, and telephone lines. Not only were these attacks designed to undermine the effectiveness of German communications during the battle, they would also force the Germans to rely on radios to communicate. Since the British had cracked most of the Germans' codes, they could monitor German radio communications and stay reasonably well informed about German troop movements and supplies. Over the next couple of weeks, Butt was extremely busy, organising attacks on German communications and convoys, as well as finding hiding places for RAF pilots who had been forced to parachute out of their planes over French territory. She also took on duties as a weapons instructor. Sensing that some of the men were embarrassed to be taught weaponry by a young girl, she told them, 'I know I am only a girl but we are short-handed. This weapon takes a bit of figuring out. But when you know it, you will be able to use it better than I can.'[16] There was also the task of finding safe houses for the group's wireless operator, since German direction-finding devices were hard at work in the area.

Eventually, Hudson decided to form a large group of armed men who could carry out damaging attacks against German units and distract the Germans from the Allies at Normandy, whose invasion appeared to have stalled. Butt and Hudson decided that the Forêt de Charnie was a logical base for this force of Resistance fighters, and soon established a camp there. Butt was an active participant in the night-time ambushes that were launched against the German convoys, impressing her counterparts with her fearlessness. Their usual technique would be to lie in wait along thickly wooded areas of a main road, making sure that there was a country road or trail nearby, to which they could escape after the attack, making a speedy exit from the area by either bike or car. As the convoy approached, the ambushers would attack the lead vehicle with Sten guns, disabling it, and then rake the rest of the convoy with gunfire and grenades before slipping away into the woods to make their escape. These ambushes, led by Butt and Hudson, were tremendously successful but required a constant supply of guns and ammunition. An arms drop was planned for the evening of 7 July 1944, but on the morning of the drop it was discovered that a group of Resistance men had been arrested on one of the roads just outside the forest. The Germans were now alerted to the fact that Resistance activity was taking place within the Charnie. Butt and Hudson set off for the forest on 8 July, stopping at a safe house a few miles from their destination. Here they learned that, under torture, one of the Resistance men had led the Germans to the site of the arms drop and a firefight had taken place. Many of the Resistance fighters were killed or taken prisoner. The group's wireless operator had managed to escape but he had been forced to leave behind his radio. Worse still, all of the arms that were parachuted in were captured by the Germans.

The loss of the radio was probably the most devastating outcome of the Charnie attack. Without contact with London, Butt and her group were unable to arrange for parachute drops of arms and supplies. There was also a shortage of money. Operating capital was necessary to provide the group members with clothing, shoes and bicycle tyres, and to purchase the 'goodwill' of local residents. A suggestion was made to approach the treasurer of the

Catholic Church in Le Mans, in the hope that, even if he did not provide the Resistance with funds, he at least would not betray them to the Gestapo. Butt approached the Abbé Chevalier and arranged a meeting between him and Sydney Hudson. Hudson managed to secure 200,000 francs of Church funds. With this money in hand, the group was able to focus its full attention on the disruption of German communications. Throughout the month of July, Butt helped to organise five groups of Resistance workers, who carried out a number of ambushes against the Germans and cut the phone lines and cables running through the district. It was also during this period that Butt once again showed her unwillingness to back down from the Germans. One day, while exiting a building in Le Mans, she discovered that a German soldier had taken her bicycle and ridden off on it. Furious, Butt followed the soldier and, upon seeing him park the bicycle and enter a shop, she promptly stole it back and continued on her way!

As the HEADMASTER network waited anxiously for the Allies to break out from the Normandy beaches, they realised that, in order to continue to work effectively, they required radio contact with London. Butt was sent off on her bicycle in an attempt to link up with someone who could provide the group with a radio. She returned empty-handed two days later, with news that the Allies were breaking through on the Normandy front. This fact was borne out when, days later, Butt and Hudson were cycling along the road and saw two German staff cars pass them. That in itself was not unusual, but when the two cars turned around and came flying back down the road Butt and Hudson braced themselves for trouble. The Germans sped right past the pair, however, and they soon learned why the Germans had been travelling so quickly. At a crossroad up ahead, an American armoured column was making its way past! Clearly the tide of the war in France was turning.

With the knowledge that the Allies were in the area, Hudson requisitioned a German staff car that their group had found abandoned and, after mounting a French flag on the front, he and Butt drove off towards the American lines. They made contact with American intelligence, and over the next several days the Resistance groups began to come out of hiding, rather secure in the knowledge that they were now behind the Allied lines. Butt, however, had a moment where she was made to feel anything but safe. Because of her habit of dining in cafés frequented by Germans, and of posing as a collaborator, a group of locals grabbed her off the street and grouped her with a number of French civilians who were suspected of working with the Germans. Women suspected of consorting with Germans usually had their heads shaved; Butt was in line for this type of treatment when someone in the Resistance recognised her and came to her rescue!

Once the Allied armies had managed to fight their way off the Normandy beaches, they began forcing the Germans back eastward through France. The Germans, with their miles of fortifications along the coast (known as the Atlantic Wall), had expected to be able to defeat any invasion army on the beaches. The Germans had little defence in depth, and once the Allied armies had broken through the coastal defences they were able to fan out behind German lines. By 31 July 1944 the Germans had been cleared out of Normandy and the Allies had advanced well inland. The Le Mans area where Butt and Hudson were operating was soon overrun by the Allied armies. Feeling that they could still be of use, Butt and Hudson offered their services to the Americans. Since they were familiar with the territory, why not send them in behind enemy lines to perform reconnaissance? The Americans accepted their offer, and both Butt and Hudson embarked on numerous undercover missions, penetrating deep behind German lines. During the end of August the pair, as well as another young man, were sent into the Falaise Pocket to discover whether or not the Germans were evacuating. The Falaise Pocket was a region in which the remains of the German Seventh army and the Fifth Panzer army were slowly being encircled by the advancing Allied troops. The encirclement had not been fully completed, and a corridor through which the Germans could escape still existed. Butt, Hudson, and their young friend drove by car into the pocket and, after scouring the countryside, they met up with a priest who informed them that the Germans were indeed evacuating. Information in hand, the trio headed back towards the American lines, only to run smack into a retreating column of German forces. Noticing a small gap in the column, Hudson accelerated and drove though the line of soldiers, making it safely back to the Americans and handing over the group's report. However, their next trip behind German lines was more eventful.

By the end of August the Americans were closing in on Paris. They were interested in learning about German troop strength on the other side of the Seine, and Butt and Hudson were sent in to reconnoitre. On 27 August, they managed to cross the river. Both possessed documents allowing them to pass as collaborators, and they crossed easily through German checkpoints. Travelling through the countryside, it appeared to Butt and Hudson that the Germans were not present in large numbers and they prepared to return to the American lines to report that it was doubtful the Germans intended to make a major stand in this area. Hanging the tricolour flag off the front of their car (to signal to the Americans that they were 'friendly'), they headed back towards the American lines. Rounding a curve in the road, however, they came face-to-face with a German patrol blocking the bridge across the Seine. Hudson accelerated hard, crashing through the patrol and racing across the bridge. The Germans opened fire, bullets ripping through the back window of the car. Butt escaped injury (however, she later discovered bullet holes through her jacket, which had been draped across the back of her seat), but Hudson was hit by ricocheting metal below his left shoulder. Making it across the bridge did not bring the pair the security they were hoping for. Each road they turned down was blockaded by Germans. Eventually they decided to abandon the car and travel on foot. However, the area was swarming with Germans, and Butt and Hudson felt that the safest course of action was to head for the town of Bar-sur-Seine, where hopefully they could blend in with the townspeople. The town appeared deserted except for German soldiers. The Germans stopped Butt and Hudson in a café and took them into custody with a small group of townsfolk. The women were soon released and Butt returned to the café where they had been arrested in order to collect Hudson's coat. She was confronted by two German soldiers, who searched her and then sexually assaulted her at gunpoint. Returning to where Hudson was being held, she handed him his coat and told him she had secured lodging in a local home for the night. She also told him about the assault, describing it as 'something rather disagreeable' and then commenting, 'Luckily they didn't discover the American passes.'[17] No more was said, but her reaction clearly illustrated that, while she may have been devastated by the assault, she, like many soldiers, had become somewhat desensitised to the violence inherent in war. Hudson could offer little support to Butt, as he was detained overnight, but he managed to escape and link up with her the next morning. The pair headed north along deserted roads, eventually crossing the Seine a day later. On the other side, they hailed an American jeep, and after showing the soldier their American passes they were taken back to American Divisional headquarters.

For Butt the war was now effectively over. Her husband Guy d'Artois, who had commanded over 3,000 Resistance fighters in central France and had also established the most formidable communications system in the whole Resistance, had reported to SOE's advanced headquarters in Paris, where he was reunited with Butt in September 1944. Butt was honest about the relationship that had developed between her and Sydney Hudson but was very clear about her desire to spend her life with d'Artois. Hudson was devastated, but respected her decision and left the couple in Paris. Shortly thereafter Butt became pregnant with her first child and left the service, travelling with her husband to Canada in December 1944, where they settled in the French-speaking province of Quebec. Butt and d'Artois eventually had six children: three boys (Robert, Michael and Guy) and three girls (Nadya, Christina and Lorraine). Butt was awarded the Member of the British Empire (MBE) and a Mention in Dispatches (when a soldier's name is listed in a report written by his or her superior officer and sent to the High Command, describing heroic action in the face of the enemy) for her service and gallantry during the war, while her husband received the Distinguished Service Order (DSO) and the French Croix de Guerre. Butt, now known by her nickname 'Tony', raised her six children and performed the duties of a military wife as d'Artois continued his career in the Armed Forces. Her daughter Nadya remembers that her mother did not speak too often about her wartime exploits, and believes that was out of sensitivity for her husband and a desire to make sure she did not 'outshine' him.[18] Always full of energy and extremely active in social situations, Butt continued to charm all who met her. Nadya describes Butt as 'a very strong mother who made all of the decisions. She was, and is, always beautifully dressed – a real clotheshorse, with her nails done and her lipstick on.'[19]

Butt, despite being charming and beautifully dressed, never lost her toughness, however. Her daughter Nadya recalls an incident where Butt jumped to the defence of one of her sons, who had been driving home with a friend when he was stopped by three men who began threatening and intimidating him. The incident occurred outside a home where Butt happened to be having dinner, and she confronted the men, hitting one of them in the face while smashing the car door on his leg. She held the other two men until police arrived on the scene. The courage, which had served her so well during the war, was clearly still in play, and as Nadya explains, 'You didn't mess with my mother.'[20]

In December 2001, Butt flew to London, England, and was reunited with her fellow agents, Nancy Wake and Sydney Hudson, who had gathered to attend the premier of the documentary *Behind Enemy Lines – The Real Charlotte Grays*. Butt and Hudson had not seen each other since the war, and those who witnessed their reunion describe it as deeply touching. The documentary detailed the stories of female agents during the Second World War, and it was an exciting opportunity for the old friends to catch up. She returned to England in March 2004 to witness her lifelong friend Wake being made a Companion of the Order of Australia, declaring proudly that 'nobody can beat you Nancy, nobody'.[21] Butt remained close to and corresponded regularly with Hudson, who published his own account of his military career (*Undercover Operator*), and died in April 2005 at the age of ninety-four. Guy d'Artois was hospitalised for the last five years of his life and Butt was his devoted caregiver, demonstrating a deep loyalty and love for her husband right until the end. He passed away in March 1999 at the Veterans Hospital in Sainte-Anne-de-Bellevue, Quebec.

Butt was one of the last surviving female SOE agents and her role in the war captured the interest of many. However, throughout her final years she declined most requests for interviews and, according to her daughter Nadya, was very concerned that her story would be distorted and 'glamorised'.[22] Relishing her role as mother and grandmother, she spent the remainder of her life living just outside the city of Montreal. In the last several years leading up to her death, she suffered from Alzheimer's but was well cared for by both her loving family and a devoted caregiver, John Tozer. Butt passed away in hospital on 21 December 2014 at the age of ninety. A funeral service was held in Hudson, Quebec, on 10 January 2015, and the outpouring of condolences revealed not only how highly Butt was regarded as a friend and neighbour, but also that her service in helping to secure the freedoms we enjoy today had not been forgotten.

Diana Rowden (1915–44)
Code Name: Paulette

Late in the afternoon of 6 July 1944, four women arrived at the Natzweiler-Struthof concentration camp, the only German extermination camp known to have been located on French soil. This fact did not bode well for the futures of the four new arrivals. The presence of the women in what was an all-male camp sparked a wave of interest among the inmates, and speculation rippled through the barracks. This interest peaked later that evening when witnesses saw the four women being led towards the crematorium. Flames shot from the crematorium chimney four times, marking each time that the oven doors were opened and closed. The women were never seen again. One of these women was Diana Rowden.

Diana Hope Rowden was born on 31 January 1915 in London, England. The First World War was just a few months old, and no one could have predicted that the newborn baby girl would eventually lose her life defending her country in a similar conflict, less than thirty years later. Her parents, Aldred Rowden (a Major in the Army) and his Scottish wife Christian, separated when she was very young. Diana, her two brothers (Maurice and Cecil) and her mother then moved to the French Riviera where she enjoyed what was, by all accounts, an idyllic childhood. The family had enough money to afford a comfortable lifestyle and, indeed, lived much of the time aboard a yacht, named the *Sans Peur* (Without Fear), sailing up and down the French and Italian Mediterranean. Diana was an extremely capable boater and enjoyed many an afternoon dozing on deck with a string tied around her toe, waiting for the jerk of a fish on her line, which she would quickly reel in and gut with relish. She was known as quite a tomboy with a sweet and reserved personality.

When Diana was a teenager, the family returned to Britain so that Diana might receive a proper boarding-school education. She attended the Manor House School, located in Limpsfield, Surrey. Diana did not particularly enjoy her Manor House experience, and was terribly homesick for the Mediterranean, but it was here that she met and befriended Elizabeth Nicholas, a woman who later wrote a book about Diana, entitled *Death Be Not Proud* in 1958. Diana's unhappiness at school was probably responsible for the impression that her personality left on Elizabeth Nicholas. Nicholas remembered Diana as a mature and introverted girl, who kept herself removed from teenage drama and who seemed to stoically endure life rather than embracing it. She was shocked, years later, to discover, during an interview with Diana's mother, that Diana had been a true tomboy who relished life on the Mediterranean, and who spent her days boating and fishing and carousing with her brothers. Upon leaving Manor House School, Diana returned with her mother to France in 1933, while her brothers remained at school in Britain. Unsure of what she wanted to do with her life, and with no romantic prospects on the horizon,

Diana enrolled at the Sorbonne to study journalism. She found that she enjoyed her studies here much more than she did at Manor House, and upon completing her programme was able to find steady work in her chosen field. Diana was working as a journalist in Paris when the Second World War broke out in 1939. Both she and her mother watched with apprehension as Germany moved against its weaker neighbours. France was invaded by Germany in May 1940. Like many English civilians who found themselves in France and facing the German invasion, Mrs Rowden evacuated quickly, securing a spot on a coal boat for the dangerous Channel crossing. Communications were a shambles during this time and Diana lost touch with her mother, discovering only later that she had made it safely back to Britain. Diana chose not to evacuate, and remained in France where she joined the Red Cross and was assigned to the ambulance service. With the Allied forces committed to stopping the German advance through the Low Countries (Belgium and the Netherlands), the German juggernaut smashed through the lightly defended Ardennes Forest and raced for the French coast. The British Expeditionary Force (BEF), which had been stationed in France, pulled back to the port of Dunkirk where, over the course of nine days, the majority of its soldiers were evacuated back to Britain. Rowden was not among the evacuees and she spent the next year witnessing the complete subjugation of her adopted country. Her position was clearly an uncomfortable one, since Britain and Germany were at war, and she was a British citizen essentially trapped in German-occupied France. For over a year she worked feverishly, endeavouring to arrange passage back to Britain. Eventually, with the help of a burgeoning

Resistance movement, Rowden made her way back to Britain by travelling a circuitous route through Spain and Portugal. After her arrival in Britain she located her family and made arrangements to share a flat with her mother in Kensington. Rowden was devastated by the German occupation of France, and had witnessed first-hand the vicious treatment of the French at the hands of the Germans. She desperately wanted to be involved in the war effort and, in September 1941, Rowden joined the Women's Auxiliary Air Force (WAAF). After three months of training she was assigned a position as Assistant Section Officer (ASO) for Intelligence Duties. An ASO was the approximate equivalent in rank to a Second Lieutenant in the Royal Air Force (RAF) and as such her position was supervisory. Rowden was posted to the Department of the Chief of Air Staff from December 1941 until July 1942 when she was promoted to Section Officer (rank equivalent Lieutenant). From there she was posted to the RAF station at Moreton-in-Marsh, which served as the home strip for many of the Wellington bombers that were used for night-time bombing runs against Germany. She remained at Moreton-in-Marsh until March 1943, and it was during her time here that Rowden was sent to an RAF convalescent home to recuperate from a minor operation. While convalescing she met Squadron Leader William Simpson, who was being treated for the multiple burns he had suffered after being shot down over France. Simpson was also working for the Special Operations Executive (SOE). Impressed by Rowden's commitment to the war effort, as well as her command of the French language, Simpson brought Rowden's file to the attention of the SOE recruiters. A memo about her recruitment, found in Rowden's personnel file, simply reads, 'Has interesting linguistic qualifications which might make her of value for operational purposes.'[1]

A background check was completed on Rowden, and SOE apparently found nothing in her past that caused them any concern. SOE sent her a formal letter indicating that they were interested in speaking with her and, on 15 March 1943, Rowden reported to Room 238 at the Hotel Victoria for a preliminary interview. Her ability to speak French, Italian and Spanish, as well as her familiarity with France, impressed the interviewer, and later that month Rowden was seconded (a military release from assigned duties to temporary duties elsewhere) from the WAAF to SOE. She signed the Official Secrets Act and was told to report for training.

All potential SOE agents had to complete an initial training course that served not only to train recruits in the subtleties of espionage and the use of explosives, codes, signals, parachutes and firearms, but also to weed out candidates who were not suited for covert operations. French was spoken almost exclusively, and instructors familiarised themselves with every aspect of each candidate agent's personality. Before leaving for her Preliminary Training course at Wanborough, Diana revealed to her mother the type of work she was being trained for, and Mrs Rowden desperately tried to dissuade her, fearing it was far too risky and worrying about losing her only daughter. The two women were very close, and Rowden struggled with her decision to leave her mother. However, Rowden had seen first-hand what the Germans were capable of, and the news stories trickling across the Channel made it very clear that the French population was suffering terribly under its German occupiers. Diana decided it was important for her to return to France and take action against the Germans, so she chose to ignore her mother's pleas. After a few weeks of Preliminary Training at Wanborough, Rowden showed enough promise to be sent up to Scotland for further paramilitary training. She did reasonably well on all her courses, and the report she received at the end of her training indicated that she was viewed as physically quite fit (though lacking in agility), and that she performed particularly well in the areas of weapons use, explosives and demolitions, and fieldcraft. Her instructors noted that she was quite skilled in both shooting and grenade throwing! There were, however, concerns about her map-reading skills and her ability to write clear and concise reports (which was odd since she had worked as a journalist); her work with signals (coding/decoding messages and wireless radio transmissions) was considered so poor that it was thought not to be worth pursuing. Her finishing report was merely adequate, stating,

> She does not seem to be of more than average intelligence and is not very quick. She tried extremely hard and was very anxious to learn. Her practical work, although often rather unimaginative, was nevertheless carried out with care. Her personality, though pleasant, is rather uninspiring. She seems confident in herself and ready to carry out any job to the best of her ability. However she has no particular powers of leadership and is not really capable of occupying an executive position but should be a reliable subordinate in carrying out a straight forward task.[2]

It was during training that she met and became close with fellow SOE recruits Robert Maloubier and Eliane Plewman. Maloubier spent many evenings socialising with Rowden during their training and remembered her as 'a sweet girl, not particularly attractive, red haired and a bit spotty, but with lovely blue eyes'.[3] Plewman and Rowden finished their security training at Beaulieu together where they were assigned a training mission called the Ninety-Six Hours Scheme. This was a training exercise set up for couriers where the students were required to reconnoitre the area around, including two English towns that they had been assigned. They also had to make arrangements to establish communications between the two towns, which involved setting up 'live' and 'dead' letter drops, sending 'veiled language' messages and recruiting possible informants. This aspect of training was extremely important since most of the female agents were used as couriers, and thus the 'passing along' or retrieval of information constituted the bulk of their work. 'Live' letter drops were locations where agents met to pass along information. Cafés, train stations and other public establishments were often used in this capacity, since agents were less likely to draw attention to themselves if they mixed among crowds. 'Dead' letter drops were physical locations (secret compartments in furniture, hollowed-out trees) where communications could be securely placed by one agent for pickup by another, thereby avoiding any contact between the agents. 'Veiled language' was a more basic substitute for code. One agent might write that he was looking forward to a wonderful birthday present on a certain date, which could mean the arrival of another SOE agent. As with her previous training, Rowden did not particularly impress her instructors with her imagination or initiative. Her performance appraisal on this exercise was not encouraging and she was heavily criticised for providing incomplete reports of her activities. Eliane Plewman, however, received a glowing report. The friendship between the two women grew, and fellow friend and SOE agent Robert Maloubier remembers many good nights sharing drinks and playing cards during their training and during the time before they were each assigned their missions. Sadly, those light-hearted times shared by the friends during the late spring of 1943 would never be repeated. Maloubier survived the war. Plewman and Rowden did not.

By early 1943 the French Resistance movement was becoming better organised and more effective in its efforts to hamper the German war effort. Acts of sabotage were taking place throughout the country, and escape lines for rescued Allied airmen were operating with much success. The British-controlled 'F' Section of SOE ('F' Section being the department of SOE that was in charge of agents sent into France) had established a number of regional Resistance networks, or circuits, designed for military intelligence-gathering purposes and to assist in Resistance efforts. In an effort to coordinate the regional pockets of Resistance workers, couriers were required to carry messages from agent to agent and group to group. Rowden was informed that she would be sent into Occupied France to act as a courier for the ACROBAT network, run by a man named John Starr. Well aware of the danger involved in being an undercover agent, she prepared her last will and testament, leaving the bulk of her small estate to her mother. While she was keen to begin her mission, Rowden was troubled about the anxiety her departure would cause her mother. She left behind instructions that if anything were to happen to her, her mother should not be told until the last possible moment. On 16 June 1943 Rowden joined two other agents, Noor Inayat Khan and Cecily Lefort, as well as the 'F' Section Chief's assistant, Vera Atkins, at Tangmere Cottage in Sussex. Lefort, code-named Alice, was assigned to act as courier for the JOCKEY network, and Khan, code-named Madeleine, was to act as a wireless operator for the CINEMA network. The group enjoyed a farewell dinner, and later that evening were transported by car to the RAF airfield. The women flew by Lysander, Khan and Lefort in one and Rowden in the other, and landed in a field deep in the heart of Occupied France, not far from the city of Angers. It was a clear, moonlit night, and the women hurried to disembark and unload the planes. Speed was imperative as the planes needed to take to the air before the Germans had time to track them. Rowden and her fellow agents were met by Henri Déricourt, a man who was ostensibly working for SOE but was later proved to be a double agent. He had with him five people, including SOE agents Jack and Francine Agazarian who would be returning to Britain aboard the Lysanders. The new passengers were quickly loaded on to the aircraft and they took off. Déricourt presented Rowden, Lefort and Khan with bicycles, and the women said their goodbyes and went their separate ways. None of the women would ever return home.

Rowden, code-named Paulette and using the name Juliette Thérèse Rondeau, travelled immediately to the town of Saint-Amour in the Jura region of France. Here she met both John Starr, the ACROBAT organiser, and his wireless operator John Young. Despite his skills as a wireless operator, Young's French was hampered by an incredibly strong northern English accent. He was encouraged to speak as little as possible, so one of Rowden's main responsibilities was to travel with Young and talk on his behalf. This put a great deal of pressure on Rowden for, although she was fluent in French, she too spoke the language with a distinctive English accent. Rowden also began her courier duties immediately. Making good use of the bicycle she had been given, she journeyed throughout the area, even going as far as Paris to retrieve agents' messages so that Young could transmit them back to Britain. Rowden was the sole link between all of the agents in the Jura region, and the Jura's only wireless operator. It was physically exhausting work, made even more difficult by the constant threat of German roadblocks and the possibility of meeting with agents who were already under surveillance by German authorities. On one of her trips to Marseille, Rowden's train was boarded by the German police who demanded to see all of the passengers' identification papers. Worried that the police might recognise that her papers were forged, Rowden locked herself in the train's bathroom until the Germans had departed. While her courier duties filled her days, Rowden's evenings were spent in fields, setting up flares and shining flashlights to guide the RAF planes to their parachute drop sites. The arms and ammunition received from these drops enabled the Resistance to inflict numerous attacks of sabotage against the Germans.

Rowden was responsible for helping to plan and for providing the explosives for a major act of sabotage against the Peugeot plant (an automotive factory that the Germans refuge in a small shop in the hamlet of Epy, owned by one of her friends in the Resistance. There she eagerly pitched in and helped in the shop, and her willingness to lend a hand was much appreciated by the shop owner Madame Rheithouse, who stated, 'I knew she was not accustomed to do such things ... she was a woman of refinement and education, but she was without vanity. She helped me in the shop because she said it would help her not be bored.'[4] Rowden spent three weeks there before joining Young, in August, at a sawmill just outside the town of Clairvaux. Isolated and in a densely wooded area, the mill seemed to be a secure base for operations. The Resistance movement was quite strong in this area and few people asked any questions. The owner of the sawmill, M. Janier-Dubry, was a strong Resistance supporter and was delighted to be providing refuge for the two British agents. Moreover, the woods surrounding the mill made Rowden feel confident that she could escape undercover if the Germans ever did show up. Rowden lodged with the Juif family, who owned part of the mill, in their beautiful Swiss-chalet-style home. The Juif and the Janier-Dubry families put themselves at considerable risk allowing the two British officers to hide there. The risk was magnified by the fact that Young was continuing to send radio transmissions from the mill, and German radio-detection vehicles were hard at work in the area. However, the Juifs and the Janier-Dubrys were quite fond of Rowden, who happily rolled up her sleeves and helped out around the house, and they were determined to keep her safe. They helped her to alter her appearance and told people she was their cousin Marcelle, who was staying with them to recover from an illness. Rowden was frustrated by having

Young's wife in order to verify his identity. The Germans immediately sent one of their own officers, in place of Benoit, to rendezvous with Rowden and Young in Lons-le-Saunier. Young received a message that a new agent had arrived in the area, and both he and Rowden were excited about the agent's arrival, hoping perhaps that he might bring news from home or some letters from loved ones. Always cautious at first, Rowden and Young arranged to meet with the man at one of the homes surrounding the sawmill. A man calling himself Benoit arrived at the mill early in the morning of 18 November 1943. He produced the letter from Young's wife, which convinced the pair to trust him, and yet Young apparently still had misgivings about the newcomer, though he chose to ignore them. This was to prove a deadly mistake.

Benoit told both Rowden and Young that he needed to go back into town to retrieve a suitcase he had left there, but indicated that he would return to the mill later in the day. Plagued by a sense of unease, Young spent the rest of the day moving his wireless transmitter to different hiding places around the mill. Rowden ventured in to Lons-le-Saunier to meet a Resistance friend, Henri Clerc, for a drink. She told him of the new agent's arrival and they were both eventually joined by Benoit at the café. Chatting and drinking together, Rowden and Clerc were quite at ease with the newcomer. Benoit quizzed them both about the situation in the area, asking questions about Gestapo activity and whether the two were afraid of being arrested. Rowden dismissed the idea of being frightened, explaining, 'The Gestapo interpreter was on our side, and tipped them off when action was to be taken.'[6] At around six o'clock in the evening of 18 November, Rowden and Benoit returned to the mill and walked up the

Top left: 1. Arisaig House, where agents were trained in guerilla warfare. (Glyn Ednie)

Above left: 2. Montagu Estate, the site of Beaulieu 'finishing school'. (The National Motor Museum, Beaulieu)

Top right: 3. Mass parachute descent. Agents had parachute training at Ringway. (J. & C. McCutcheon Collection)

Right: 4. Grendon Hall was used by the SOE for training, and for receiving messages from agents. (Andy Gryce)

5. Inverie Bay, the location of Wake's all-male explosives training group. (Peter Van den Bossche)

6. Sten gun, carried by many of the female agents. (J. & C. McCutcheon Collection)

7. Thame Park, the wireless school where Noor Inayat Khan was trained in coding and ciphering. (David Harrison)

8. The Rings, the instructors' house on the Montagu Estate. (The National Motor Museum, Beaulieu)

Top left: 9. Violette Szabo, who enlisted as a secret agent to seek revenge on the Germans and was executed by a single gunshot to the back of the head at Ravensbrück concentration camp. (Susan Ottaway)

Top right: 10. Etienne and Violette Szabo on their wedding day at Aldershot on 21 August 1940, less than a month after meeting. (Susan Ottaway)

Above: 11. Free French Forces parade on Bastille Day 1940, the very day that Violette met her future husband, Etienne. (J. & C. McCutcheon Collection)

Top left: 12. Violette Szabo's ID card, with her assumed name Corinne Reine Leroy. (David Harrison)

Top right: 13. Violette Szabo's George Cross. Violette was the first woman to be awarded this honour. The medal was accepted by seven-year-old Tania Szabo on 28 January 1947 on behalf of her late mother. (Susan Ottaway)

Middle: 14. The entrance to the Violette Szabo Museum, located in Herefordshire, England, and run by Rosemary E. Rigby. (Pauline Eccles)

Left: 15. The Violette Szabo Museum. (Bob Embleton)

Top left: 16. Nancy Wake, the Allies' most decorated servicewoman of the Second World War. (Special Forces Club)

Top right: 17. Rue Henri Fiocca in Marseille, named after Nancy Wake's wealthy first husband and love of her life, whom she married in November 1940. (Jason Menzies and Lucy Allen)

Middle: 18. The Auvergne region as Nancy would have seen it when parachuting in on 31 April 1944. (Raphaël Vanleynseele)

Right: 19. Nancy Wake's ashes were scattered in a wooded area near Verneix in March 2013. The service was very well attended, and was followed by a drinks reception at the mayor's office. (Janette Brown)

20. Gibraltar Barn, RAF Tempsford, from where agents flew to France. (Peter Skynner)

21. Gibraltar Barn plaque. (Peter Skynner)

22. Grignon Agricultural College, just west of Versailles, the working headquarters of the PROSPER network for whom Noor Inayat Khan acted as a wireless operator. (Direction de la communication AgroParisTech)

23. Supply containers dropped in the Vercors plateau, where Granville worked. On 14 July 1944 hundreds of Allied planes dropped over a thousand containers of supplies into the region. (Peter Skynner)

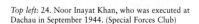

A LA MÉMOIRE DE
NOOR INAYAT KHAN
dite 'MADELEINE'
George Cross, Croix de querre
Héroïne de la Résistance
1914 – 1944

Top left: 24. Noor Inayat Khan, who was executed at Dachau in September 1944. (Special Forces Club)

Top right: 25. Noor Inayat Khan memorial bust in Gordon Square, London. (Paul Farmer)

Above: 26. Noor Inayat Khan memorial plaque, Grignon. (David Harrison)

Right: 27. WAAFs loading a tug with barrage balloons. Khan worked with various barrage ballon groups. (J. & C. McCutcheon Collection)

Top: 28. Sonia Butt in her uniform at Versailles. (Nadya Murdoch)

Left: 29. Sonia and Guy on their wedding day. (Nadya Murdoch)

Above: 30. Sonia d'Artois in July 2011 at her grandson's wedding. (Nadya Murdoch)

Opposite top left: 31. A female parachutist preparing to jump. (J. & C. McCutcheon Collection)

Opposite top right: 32. Liberator aircraft. Wake, Szabo and Butt were flown to France in this kind of plane. (J. & C. McCutcheon Collection)

Opposite middle: 33. Lysander aircraft. Khan and Rowden were flown to France in this type of plane. (J. & C. McCutcheon Collection)

Opposite bottom: 34. Halifax aircraft, in which Granville travelled. (J. & C. McCutcheon Collection)

35. The crematoriums at Dachau, where Noor Inayat Khan was executed. (Robyn Walker)

36. Diana Rowden, who was executed at Natzweiler-Struthof concentration camp. (Susan Ottaway)

IN PROUD AND LOVING MEMORY OF
DIANA HOPE ROWDEN
S/O. W. A. A. F. KILLED IN NATZWEILER
CONCENTRATION CAMP 6TH JULY
1944, AGED 29, BELOVED ONLY
DAUGHTER OF ALDRED CLEMENT
ROWDEN AND CHRISTIAN ROWDEN
LOWICKS, TILFORD.

GREATER LOVE HATH NO MAN THAN THIS
THAT A MAN LAY DOWN HIS LIFE FOR HIS FRIENDS

37. Diana Rowden memorial plaque, All Saints church, Tilford. (John Horrocks and the Tilford Bach Society)

Top left: 38. Odette Sansom, one of only four agents arrested in France who returned home. (Susan Ottaway)

Top right: 39. Vera Atkins, assistant to Maurice Buckmaster; she travelled to Europe after the Second World War attempting to track down what had happened to the agents who had not returned. (David Harrison)

Middle: 40. Odette and Peter Churchill on their wedding day in 1947. (David Harrison)

Right: 41. Odette Hallowes's grave in Burvale Cemetery, Hersham, Surrey. (Kevin Brazier)

YVONNE MARIE ROSE
BRAILLY
1890 – 1960

ODETTE MARIE CELINE
HALLOWES
Née Brailly
GC MBE Légion d'Honneur
1912 – 1995

GEOFFREY MACLEOD
HALLOWES

42. These railway sidings and the gasworks have been bombed as a result of Resistance intelligence from the area around Rouen, where Violette Szabo operated. (J. & C. McCutcheon Collection)

43. The gates of Natzweiler-Struthof, the only German concentration camp located on French soil; this was where Diana Rowden was executed. (Karen Bayley-Ewell)

44. The crematorium at Natzweiler-Struthof concentration camp. (Ian Macdonald)

45. Fresnes prison, outside of Paris, where Szabo, Rowden and Sansom were held before being transported to other prisons or concentration camps. (Lionel Allorge)

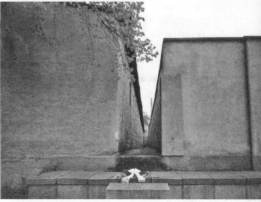

Top left: 46. A portable wireless. The job of wireless operator was hazardous and physically exhausting. (J. & C. McCutcheon Collection)

Top right: 47. No. 84 Avenue Foch, the infamous Gestapo counter-intelligence headquarters, where Szabo, Khan, Rowden and Sansom were interrogated. (David Harrison)

Middle: 48. Execution Alley, Ravensbrück concentration camp, where Violette Szabo was murdered along with Lilian Rolfe and Denise Bloch. (David Harrison)

Right: 49. Vichy town hall, the seat of the Vichy government in the Free Zone. (Jean-Louis Zimmermann)

The Gaol   Aylesbury No 88

Above left: 50. Women who collaborated with the Germans in France could expect to have their hair shaved off and a swastika drawn on their forehead. (J. & C. McCutcheon Collection)

Above right: 51. Mathilde Carré, who acted as a double agent and was found guilty of treason. (Susan Ottaway)

Middle: 52. Aylesbury prison, where Mathilde Carré was held following her arrest. (Buckinghamshire Historical Society)

Left: 53. Dachau memorial plaque for Noor Inayat Khan. (Robyn Walker)

Here in Dachau on the 12th of September 1944 four young Woman Officers of the British Forces attached to Special Operations Executive were brutally murdered and their bodies cremated. They died as gallantly as they had served the Resistance in France during the common struggle for freedom from tyranny.

Mrs YOLANDE E M BEEKMAN (née Unternahrer)
Croix de Guerre avec Étoile de Vermeil
Women's Auxiliary Air Force seconded to Women's Transport Service (FANY)

Miss MADELEINE DAMERMENT
Légion d'Honneur   Croix de Guerre avec Étoile de Vermeil
Women's Transport Service (FANY)

Miss NOORUNISA INAYAT KHAN
George Cross   Member of the Most Excellent Order of the British Empire
Mentioned in Despatches   Croix de Guerre avec Étoile de Vermeil
Women's Auxiliary Air Force seconded to Women's Transport Service (FANY)

Mrs ELIANE S PLEWMAN (née Browne Bartroli)
Croix de Guerre avec Étoile de Vermeil
Women's Transport Service (FANY)

"But the souls of the righteous are in the hand of God, and there shall no torment touch them"

Above left: 54. Christine Granville, England's longest-serving female agent of the Second World War. (Special Forces Club)

Above right: 55. Christine Granville's grave. Granville was murdered by her stalker, Dennis Muldowney, on 15 June 1952. She is buried at St Mary's Roman Catholic Cemetery in north-west London. (Iain MacFarlaine)

Below: 56. Vercors Plateau, where Christine Granville operated with Francis Cammaerts and a large French Resistance group. (Peter Skynner)

cobblestone road to the Juif home. Unbeknown to Rowden, Benoit was flashing a torch signal behind his back to allow the German police to follow his trail. A member of the Resistance who was supposed to meet with Rowden, Young and Benoit spotted several German police cars tailing Rowden, and dashed off to warn the others. Unfortunately Diana had no such warning. German police burst through the doors of the Juif farmhouse, startling Young, who was playing chess, and Madame Juif, who was cooking dinner. Rowden, who had been chatting with Benoit, held her nerve as the twenty or so *Feldgendarmerie* (German military police charged with policing matters in occupied territory), armed with machine guns, stormed the house. Both Rowden and Young were immediately arrested and taken to the Lons-le-Saunier police station. Rowden was locked in a cell by herself, but could hear Young's cries as he was tortured during his interrogation. He was eventually executed at Mauthausen on 6 September 1944. Later that evening, the Germans returned to the sawmill to search all the homes more thoroughly. However, in their absence, the Resistance had sneaked in and removed Young's wireless set.

Rowden was taken to Paris the next day and kept at the infamous Avenue Foch for two weeks, during which she was interrogated by German counter-intelligence. Upon her arrival, Rowden was shocked to see her former organiser, John Starr, comfortably situated and apparently collaborating with the Germans. Starr had, in an effort to save himself, agreed to 'assist' the Germans in minor ways, either by making other agents feel more comfortable or by using his considerable artistic skills to create artwork for them. He did enjoy quite a comfortable period at Avenue

Foch but was eventually transferred to a concentration camp where he managed to survive the war. Captured agents who passed through Avenue Foch definitely questioned his loyalty, and after the war an investigation was launched into his relationship with the Germans. However, there was not enough evidence to prosecute him and no criminal charges were ever laid.

Unlike Starr, Rowden had no interest in working with the Germans. Despite intensive interrogation she told them nothing, and the Germans finally realised that she was a useless source of information. Rowden left her mark on the walls of 84 Avenue Foch with an inscription, discovered by the Allies in October 1944, which read, 'S/O D. H. Rowden No: 4193 W.A.A.F arrived 22.11.43 and left 5.12.43.' She was eventually transferred to Fresnes prison on 5 December 1943, and it was during her time here that she earned the gratitude of fellow SOE agents Odette Sansom and Peter Churchill. Sansom and Churchill were lovers, and been caught together the previous April. Churchill has often told the story about the moment he spotted Odette in a holding pen at Avenue Foch, and, though under guard, slipped over to her so that they could exchange a few words. He recalled,

I slipped up close to Odette, and as she slipped up close to me with her back to the sentry, a girl I had never seen before but who was patently English to her fingertips, stood between me and the guard so that he could not see my mouth moving. Despite my anxiety not to miss a second of the golden opportunity to speak with Odette, I was nevertheless instinctively conscious of the girl's unselfish act which included a delicacy of feeling that made her turn about and face the German so as not to butt in on our privacy. I could not imagine what this refined creature with reddish hair was doing in our midst. 'Who is she?' I asked Odette. 'Diana Rowden,' she replied, 'one of us.'[7]

It was a brave move that Peter Churchill never forgot.

On 13 May 1944, Rowden, Yolande Beekman, Madeleine Damerment, Eliane Plewman, Andrée Borrel, Vera Leigh, Sonia Olschanezky and Odette Sansom (all SOE agents) were brought from Fresnes prison to Avenue Foch, where they spent the afternoon together. It was a beautiful day, and the women enjoyed the chance to catch up and share their experiences. Odette Sansom remembered the women sharing a lipstick and having tea, and John Starr even dropped in and gave the women some chocolate. Later that afternoon the agents were chained together and transported by train to a civil prison at Karlsruhe. Conditions there, while not comfortable, were not horrendous. Food was adequate, and the female prisoners were expected to do manual labour, such as sewing and food preparation. The women were separated and placed in cells with German civil prisoners. Each cell was long and narrow, and had a spyhole in the door. There was a toilet, a folding table and two plank beds with straw-filled mattresses. A bell rang at 6.30 a.m. to start the day, and all of the prisoners were expected to wash and tidy their cell. Breakfast would be pushed through a hatch in their cell door and then the women would line up for inspection. Weather permitting, there would be a half hour of exercise in the prison yard, during which the prisoners were expected to walk around in two circles, and then their time after lunch was devoted to work. Dinner was followed by an early bedtime. Had they remained there, the women may have survived the war. Yet early in the morning on 6 July 1944, Diana Rowden, Andrée Borrel, Vera Leigh and Sonia Olschanezky were told to prepare for a journey. Two men from the Gestapo escorted them on the 90-mile trip to the Natzweiler concentration camp.

Natzweiler has the dubious distinction of being the only German concentration camp located on French soil. Located in the French province of Alsace, the camp was surrounded by majestic mountains. The Nazis opened the camp in 1941, and by the time Rowden passed through its gates Natzweiler had already claimed thousands of victims. On 6 July 1944, it claimed four more. Rowden, Leigh, Borrel and Olschanezky arrived at the camp during the late afternoon. Prisoners Brian Stonehouse (SOE wireless operator, who was arrested in October 1943) and Albert Guérisse (organiser of an escape line for Allied pilots, who was arrested in March 1943) both witnessed the four women being brought into the camp. The fact that the women had been brought to Natzweiler, which was a men's camp, sparked rumours among the male inmates that the women were there to be executed. Later in the evening, a curfew was imposed on the camp, which required all male inmates to be locked down in their barracks with the windows closed. Clearly something was afoot, and the Germans wanted as few witnesses as possible. According to eyewitness statements the women were taken, one by one, out of their cells to the crematorium, where they were told that they were to receive an injection against typhus. Instead they were each injected with phenol. Phenol is an extremely toxic chemical, and the Germans found these injections, whether they be

War Office, saying that London had been 'out of touch with Diana, and that under the circumstances she must be considered missing'.[10] This was followed by a letter in December 1945, which stated, 'Diana was very keen on this work, and the only aspect of it which troubled her considerably was the thought of the anxiety which you would suffer if you lacked all news ... we now know that she was unhappily arrested towards the end of November 1943.'[11] Mrs Rowden received a final letter, in April 1946, which stated, 'The girls were or appeared to be in good health and bore themselves with courage and were utterly defiant in their attitude to the S.S. ... all who came into contact with Diana during the time of her imprisonment have spoken most highly of her courage and morale.'[12]

Diana Rowden was twenty-nine years old when she died. No single-subject biography has yet been written about her life, nor has she been the subject of any movies or television programs. Perhaps this is because she was not quite as glamorous as some of her counterparts. Yet her bravery and devotion to duty mark her as one of SOE's finest agents. Maurice Buckmaster, head of SOE's French Section, certainly felt Diana's story needed to be remembered; in 1957 he told author Elizabeth Nicholas that 'the stories of some others ... had to a certain degree eclipsed her magnificent record'.[13] In France, Rowden was posthumously awarded the Croix de Guerre and appointed a Chevalier de la Légion d'honneur. In Britain she was made a Member of the Order of the British Empire (MBE) and Mentioned in Dispatches. Rowden's name has been registered with the Scottish National War Memorial located in Edinburgh Castle and with the Runnymede Memorial in Surrey. Her name can also be found inscribed on the Valençay SOE Memorial, which was unveiled in 1991 on the anniversary of the first 'F' Section agent being sent in to France. This memorial's Roll of Honour lists the names of all SOE agents who died for French freedom. The FANY Memorial at St Paul's church, Knightsbridge, also bears her name. A watercolour of Diana Rowden and her three comrades, painted by former SOE agent Brian Stonehouse, now hangs in the Special Forces Club in London, England. At Natzweiler concentration camp, now open to the public as a historical site, a simple plaque hangs on the wall of the crematorium, commemorating the lives of Diana Rowden and her fellow agents:

> '*À la mémoire des quatre femmes britanniques et françaises parachutées exécutées dans ce camp*'
> Borrel, Andrée
> Leigh, Vera
> Olschanezky, Sonia
> Rowden, Diana

Finally, if one looks carefully, a small plaque memorialising Rowden can be found between two stained-glass windows on the inside wall of Tilford church in Surrey. Diana Rowden is remembered.

Odette Sansom (1912–95)
Code Name: Lise

Odette Sansom made things happen. Not content to be a mere spectator in life, she went after what she wanted and, through the sheer force of her personality and her unending resourcefulness, she was usually successful. Throughout her life she seemed to have set a series of goals for herself, and one by one she achieved them. After her capture by the Germans in 1943, Sansom's only goal was to endure and survive the horrors that awaited her. Of the sixteen FANY (First Aid Nursing Yeomanry) and WAAF (Women's Auxiliary Air Force) agents that were arrested in France, only four returned home. One of these women was Odette Sansom.

Odette Marie Céline Brailly was born 28 April 1912 in Amiens, France, to Yvonne and Gaston Brailly. A younger brother, Louis, followed a year later. Odette's life was touched by war very early on, with the outbreak of the First World War in 1914. The Germans had launched their western attack by swinging down through Belgium and into France, and Odette's home town of Amiens lay directly in the path of the German war machine. Heavy bombardment by the Germans greatly damaged the city of Amiens, and German occupation forces moved in during March 1914.

Her father, who was employed at the local bank, joined the French army, and his military career was marked by a number of acts of extreme heroism. In October 1918, Sergeant Brailly was stationed at Verdun, and discovered that two of the men in his platoon were missing. He raced back to the front line, and found his two wounded comrades. Attempting to drag both men to safety, Sergeant Brailly was killed by a direct hit from a German shell, a month before the Armistice was signed. Brailly was eventually awarded the Croix de Guerre and the Médaille Militaire for his brave actions on that fateful day.

Just prior to Brailly's death, British General Haig launched a massive Allied offensive against the Germans in Amiens, sending the German armies reeling into retreat. British soldiers billeted at the Brailly home while the Allied armies continued their push towards Germany. Six-year-old Odette enjoyed the attentions of the soldiers and the treats they shared with her. She also missed her father. Odette's formative years were marked by fear and tragedy, and by the end of the war she had developed two things. The first was an affection for British soldiers; the second was a gritty determination to survive. Moreover, the seed for her later success as an undercover agent was planted, early on, by her grandfather. In a 1986 interview, Sansom recalled how each Sunday, after church, she and her brother would walk with her mother and grandparents to her father's grave. Her grandfather told her many times that 'there is going to be another war. It will be your duty, both of you, to do as well as your father did.'[1]

Sansom listened to those words for years, and they had a deep impact on her future character development.

Odette was a sickly child, suffering from both polio, which for a time both blinded and paralysed her, and rheumatic fever. Believing that the Normandy sea air would improve her overall health, Odette's mother, Yvonne, relocated the family to Boulogne, where Odette spent countless hours hiking, and exploring the Normandy coast and countryside. As she grew older, Odette blossomed into a beautiful and vivacious young woman. She was educated at the Convent of Sainte-Thérèse, where the nuns noted in her school reports that Odette was quite bright and had a good sense of humour, but that she also demonstrated the tendency to be quite petulant and obstinate.[2] Odette left school at age eighteen, and a year later married Roy Sansom, an Englishman whom she met while he was visiting France. Ironically, he also happened to be the son of one of the officers who had been billeted with the Brailly family during the First World War. Roy Sansom worked in the hotel industry, and he and his bride eventually settled in London. Odette bore three daughters – Francoise in 1932, Lily in 1934 and Marianne in 1936 – and devoted the next several years to motherhood and keeping house. She also kept abreast of current events, and watched with apprehension as the clouds of war once again appeared over Europe. The German armies were once more on the move. One by one, Austria, Czechoslovakia, Poland, Denmark and Norway fell before the German onslaught. From her home in Kensington, Sansom, along with the rest of the world, watched breathlessly to see if France and Britain could halt the German advance. On 10 May 1940, the Germans smashed through the Ardennes Forest, battering Allied defences and forcing the French and British back to the sea. By 16 June, France had surrendered, and Sansom was already giving thought to how she could best assist the war effort.

Following the evacuation of the British Expeditionary Force (BEF) from the beaches of Dunkirk, which took place from 26 May to 3 June 1940, the British suffered several months of punishing air attacks by the German Luftwaffe, a time which became known as the Battle of Britain. Sansom and her daughters spent many terrifying nights rushing to the air-raid shelter at the end of their garden. Like many English families, the Sansoms eventually packed up and left London for safer accommodation in rural Somerset. Sansom spent the next couple of years waiting for news of her mother, Yvonne, and her brother, Louis, while tending to both her girls and her mother-in-law. Her days were filled with domestic tasks, as well as fundraising for the war effort and knitting clothing for both her own children and the fighting forces. It was during this time that the British government put out a call for citizens to hand over any personal photographs they might have of the French coastline or of French towns and cities. Since the Luftwaffe had control of the air over France, aerial reconnaissance by the Royal Air Force (RAF) was extremely difficult. The photographs provided by British citizens were invaluable for planning RAF bombing operations, and ultimately in assisting in the preparations for the Allied invasion of Europe. Sansom had numerous snapshots of the French coast and of her home town of Amiens, so she provided these photographs to the British government, mailing them, by accident, to the Navy and believing she would never see her photographs again. By sending in her pictures (which the Navy had forwarded to the Army), Sansom caught the attention of the newly formed Special Operations Executive (SOE).

Opinions were mixed with regard to whether or not Sansom would make a suitable candidate for SOE. As the mother of three young children, some felt that her first duty should be to her family and that, if captured, she might fold very quickly before interrogators in an effort to survive for the sake of her children. Others, however, felt that she was an ideal candidate, as she was young, attractive, French-speaking and familiar with large areas of France. A decision was made to invite her for an interview. She received a letter thanking her for her photographs and asking her to attend a meeting in London. Thinking she was going to be given back her photographs, Sansom agreed to travel to London, and met with Captain Selwyn Jepson on Friday 10 July 1942 at the Hotel Victoria on Northumberland Avenue. He was favourably impressed with Sansom, writing at the bottom of her personal information sheet, 'Direct-minded and courageous. God help the Nazis if we can get her near enough to them. S.J.'[3] When Jepson asked her if she would be willing to do some work for the war effort, Sansom was hesitant. She offered to do some translating or some letter writing to French soldiers, for she truly believed she had an obligation to contribute, but she made it clear that, due to her family obligations, she could only participate in a limited way. The facts that her father had been killed by the Germans during the First World War and that her mother was, at the time, suffering under the German occupation of France played heavily on her mind, but she was determined to put her children first.

Sansom returned home to her girls in Somerset, but

over the course of the next several weeks she became more convinced that she needed to be a more active participant in the war effort. News she received from France upset her terribly – her mother had been forced from her home, friends had been arrested, and her brother had been wounded and was lying in a military hospital. In a 1986 interview Sansom recalled,

> I felt terrible ... I am in England ... I am in what I consider the safety of beautiful Somerset with my children, under those lovely trees ... Am I going to be satisfied to accept this ... that other people are going to suffer, get killed, die because of this war, and trying to get freedom for my children, let's face it. Am I supposed to accept this sacrifice that other people are making without lifting a finger?[4]

Sansom received another letter from Captain Jepson, requesting a second interview. Jepson told her they had made enquiries about her in both England and France, and had been extremely satisfied with what they had uncovered about her. Sansom at first was livid that they had been making enquiries about her, wondering what exactly about her character had compelled them to do this. Once she calmed down, Jepson explained that she had been identified as a potential candidate to be trained as an undercover agent. Sansom was horrified at the thought, protesting that she didn't have the brains or the physical capabilities for such work. Despite her vehement protests, Jepson asked that she keep an open mind and consider the possibility. For weeks Odette thought about what had been proposed to her. Finally, she contacted Jepson and offered to complete the training course, sure that her inadequacies would be discovered and they would see that she was not suitable secret agent material. That way, she reasoned, she would know that she had at least tried, and, confident that she would be rejected, felt satisfied that the decision would be taken out of her hands. Bolstered by the support of her husband, who, although not keen to have his wife enter the service, did not try to influence her decision either way, Sansom placed her girls in a convent school in Essex, telling them that she was joining the forces and may be sent as far away as Scotland. She kissed her family goodbye and reported to SOE for training.

Sansom joined the First Aid Nursing Yeomanry (FANY) and was sent on a training course that included physical fitness, the use of firearms, surveillance and unarmed combat. She was a capable student but not necessarily the perfect candidate for undercover work. Her finishing report, a copy of which still exists in her personnel file, reads as follows:

> Has enthusiasm and seems to have absorbed the teaching given in the course. She is, however, impulsive and hasty in her judgments and has not quite the clarity of mind which is desirable in subversive activity. She seems to have little experience of the outside world. She is excitable and temperamental, although she has a certain determination. A likeable character and gets on well with most people. Her main asset is her patriotism and keenness to do something for France; her main weakness is a complete unwillingness to admit that she could ever be wrong.[5]

Interestingly, the Chief Instructor of the SOE agents, Major

Oliver Brown, also doubted Sansom's suitability, but not for the same reasons as her final report mentioned. Brown did not find her excitable and temperamental at all, stating in a 1992 interview that 'Odette was very, very demure ... in fact I wondered if Odette would ever make it actually ... I thought she'd turn it in but she didn't ... she was intent, she was a very intent person in those days ... I think she still is.'[6] Major Buckmaster, head of SOE's French Section, was disappointed in Sansom's report, and met with her to discuss her instructors' observations. Over the course of her training, Sansom had become much more confident in her abilities to perform the job of an undercover agent. Although she was still aware of her physical limitations, she felt that mentally she would be able to endure quite a lot. Her growing confidence, combined with her increasing knowledge of the desperate conditions the French were facing under German occupation, made her determined to become an undercover operative. She was devastated that her report was not wholly satisfactory, and begged for the opportunity to prove herself. Buckmaster, either impressed by Sansom's sincerity and determination or feeling the pressure from the need to get more couriers into the field, agreed to send her into France.

Given the operational code name Lise, a whole new identity was created for Sansom. Her new name was Odette Métayer, and she was to play the part of a widowed working-class seamstress. Deciding to send Sansom into France and actually getting her into France were two entirely different things, however. It became almost a comedy of errors, as every time a plan was made for her transportation something seemed destined to go terribly wrong. Originally, the plan was to have Odette travel to France on a submarine, but the submarine commanders refused to have a woman aboard their vessel. SOE's next thought was to send her in by air, but this was marked by a series of mishaps. The first attempt resulted in a collision with another aircraft as Sansom taxied down the runway. The second was called off when SOE received news that her reception committee had been captured by the Germans and executed. A third attempt, by seaplane, was turned back due to inclement weather, and the fourth try resulted in a crash due to engine failure just after take-off. Sansom and the crew were able to evacuate the plane, but Sansom was definitely getting the sense that air travel was not the best option to get her into France, stating, 'Everytime I got on plane, something went wrong with it, and I was costing them a lot of money.'[7]

Finally, in October 1942 Sansom was transported aboard a troopship to Gibraltar, where she boarded a felucca (a type of sailboat) to Antibes. Her assignment was to join a new Resistance circuit operating in the Burgundy region of France, and she was well aware of the dangers she faced. Prior to her departure, Sansom had a charcoal-grey flannel suit made, and when asked by Vera Atkins, Buckmaster's assistant, why she had selected that particular colour Sansom replied, 'Well, you see, when I go to prison it will be very useful because it won't show the dirt.'[8] Sansom drew some sense of security from the thought that she would be working mostly on her own as part of her new assignment. However, upon her arrival on the French Riviera, where she was to pick up the papers that would allow her to cross over the demarcation line between occupied and unoccupied France, she was commandeered to act as a courier for the

SPINDLE circuit, which was headed by Peter Churchill. This alarmed Sansom, as she knew it would involve working with a large Resistance group, and the potential for security leaks would increase significantly, but she was determined not to let Buckmaster down. Churchill was fascinated by his new courier, who earned his immediate respect by demanding to be put to work virtually from the moment she arrived. Determined to test the newcomer's mettle, Churchill ordered Sansom to Marseille to pick up a suitcase. Without hesitation, Sansom, unfamiliar with the city of Marseille but knowing that it was teeming with Germans, boarded a train to begin her mission. When she was forced to spend the evening in Marseille, her accommodation turned out to be a brothel. She endured this indignity without complaint. Upon returning to Churchill, he requested that she cycle across the region with a note for one of the group's contacts. Sansom had never been on a bicycle before in her life, but she accepted the assignment, returning bloody and bruised from the numerous falls she had taken. Churchill was impressed by Sansom's willingness to take on any assignment no matter how dangerous or how morally uncomfortable. He also delighted in her ladylike manner – she neither smoked nor drank and the best expletive she could muster was a resounding 'Zut'!

The SPINDLE circuit arranged and coordinated airdrops of arms and explosives to members of the French Resistance. The French Riviera was located in Vichy France (the unoccupied area) and, although German control of the area was more or less understood, there had been no significant German presence in the zone. One notable exception was the German Gestapo agents who tracked security of the CARTE organisation had been compromised, and that SPINDLE workers were to avoid all contact with CARTE members. Sansom had remained behind in France, and Churchill had left her in charge of the circuit. Along with her courier duties, she was now responsible for arranging and supervising parachute deliveries of arms and equipment. During Churchill's absence, Sansom was approached by a German officer who indicated that he wanted to defect to the Allies. He asked for a transmitting set and a code so that he might contact London to arrange for transport out of France. Sansom was shocked at the candid nature of this request and was immediately suspicious. Her instincts were correct, as the German officer was actually Sergeant Hugo Bleicher of the Abwehr, which was the German military intelligence organisation. Bleicher was one of the Abwehr's most effective agents. With his superb command of numerous languages, and his ingratiating manner, Bleicher had infiltrated and brought the destruction of several Resistance groups, including the PROSPER circuit. Dozens of agents were arrested and died as a result of Bleicher's work. Tragically, one of the less security-conscious members of the CARTE organisation was not as astute as Sansom. The individual told Bleicher some of the names of the agents working in the Annecy area, including Sansom and Churchill. Sansom asked her wireless operator to radio to London and explain the German officer's request. London radioed back that she was to disband the circuit and break off all contact with the German officer. Sansom got busy, travelling throughout the region warning as many people she could find that they needed to lie low or leave the area. One such person was a young Englishman code-named Roger, who was staying in a hotel in Saint-Jorioz. Roger left the area immediately following Sansom's warning and was, in fact, British agent Francis Cammaerts. Later on, his life was saved by another female SOE agent, Christine Granville. Sansom continued to distribute money and orders to the couriers, and located a safe hiding place for the group's wireless operator, Arnaud. She also arranged Churchill's reception committee for when he parachuted back into France on 16 April 1943. Sansom met him at the drop site, and Churchill was elated to see her but dismayed that she had remained in the area. They travelled to a local hotel where Churchill explained the latest instructions from London and warned Sansom that they needed to break off contact with the CARTE group. Unfortunately, it was too late. The next evening Bleicher and a detachment of Italian troops raided the hotel where Sansom and Churchill were staying. Sansom was grabbed in the hallway, and when she refused to take them to Churchill a gun was unceremoniously jabbed into her back. Knowing the hotel was surrounded, and worried that if she screamed Churchill might try to escape through a window and be shot, Sansom calmly led the Gestapo to Churchill's room. Churchill was dragged from his bed and arrested. In the commotion that ensued, Sansom managed to grab Churchill's wallet, which contained several decoded messages as well as thousands of francs. She managed to hide the wallet under the seat of the car that transported the couple to the local barracks.

The Gestapo handed Sansom and Churchill over to the Italians, who treated them quite well. Despite being kept in separate rooms, the two were able to exchange messages. After a few days in the custody of the Italians, both Sansom and Churchill were loaded on to a truck. Sansom was upset by Churchill's physical appearance (he had been beaten following an escape attempt, sustaining a broken finger and facial abrasions) and she begged him not to take such risks. She gave him cigarettes that she had accepted from her captors, and slipped some eggs into his pack so that he might have food if his rations were withheld. Hoping that Peter Churchill's last name (shared with the British Prime Minister) might buy them some security, Sansom and Churchill concocted a cover story that they were married and that Churchill was in fact the nephew of Prime Minister Winston Churchill. They travelled together, first to Turin, then Nice, and then to Toulon, where the Italians turned them over to the Germans. A truck transported the pair to Marseille, and then they travelled by train to Paris where they were transferred to Fresnes prison. Sansom promised Churchill that, while he would always be on her mind, each night at six o'clock she would specifically turn her thoughts to him. He promised to do the same.

Sansom endured her time at Fresnes with stoic optimism. On at least two occasions, she was allowed to meet with Churchill and she saved portions of her rations to share with him. However, for the majority of her time in Fresnes, Sansom was kept in solitary confinement, with the words '*Grande Criminale Pas de Privilèges*' affixed to her cell door. She received less food than other prisoners, and was not allowed to shower or to have any contact with other inmates. In an effort to keep up her spirits, Sansom communicated with her fellow prisoners through the window in her cell. This helped to pass the time but did have some rather nasty repercussions. One evening, a German wardress came into her cell and smacked Sansom twice on the face, accusing her of speaking with others through the window. Sansom was so incensed at this false accusation (for, although she spoke frequently through the window, she was actually innocent on this occasion) that she demanded to speak with the prison captain, giving her name as Mrs Churchill. The captain came to her cell, and Sansom was quite clear about her disgust at the way in which she had been treated. Full of apologies, the German captain was dismayed that Sansom might think poorly of the Germans. In an effort to 'make things right' he offered to send a parcel to Churchill, as well as a message that Sansom was all right. The captain followed through on his promises and reinforced, at least in Sansom's mind, that using the name Churchill had been a very good idea!

Sansom was taken numerous times to Avenue Foch (German counter-intelligence headquarters), where she convinced the Germans that 'her husband' was merely an innocent bystander and that she alone was involved in espionage activities. She took full responsibility for all of the resistance activities in Annecy. The Germans apparently believed her, and ceased interrogating Peter Churchill. Instead, they focused on Sansom, repeatedly questioning her as to the whereabouts of her wireless operator Arnaud and the British officer named Roger. Sansom revealed nothing, and endured horrific torture, including being burned on her back with a hot iron and having her toenails torn out. The Germans quite often found someone of a prisoner's own nationality to commit the torture, in the belief that the prisoner could then never say they had been tortured by the Germans. Sansom remembered her torturer as a young, handsome Frenchman, and during their sessions she often tried to shame him. The man clearly lacked any conscience but his efforts were wasted on his charge as Sansom simply refused to break. Sansom was the only person who knew the whereabouts of Arnaud and Roger, and her refusal to reveal this information undoubtedly saved their lives. She was both defiant and dismissive of the Germans, believing this attitude garnered some of level of respect from her captors, as well as allowing her to maintain her own dignity. The Germans finally tired of their efforts to break her having come to the conclusion that she would give them no information. Sansom was condemned to death in June 1943, but remained at Fresnes prison in solitary confinement for over a year. Her spirit still unbroken, she even managed to find some dark humour in her predicament. When her sentence was read to her at Avenue Foch, Sansom discovered she had been condemned to death twice, once for France and once for Britain. Her immediate thought was, 'For which country will I die? I shall never know.'[9] The effects of Sansom's incarceration inevitably took their toll, however. Her tortured feet had never been properly tended to, and the lack of proper food and medical attention left her weak and in constant pain. In October 1943, Sansom was moved to a shared cell, with a French woman named Simone Herail. Herail was shocked by Sansom's condition and, in a statement given after the war, recalled,

I knew and lived with Miss Odette Sansom from 15 October 1943 to 11 January 1944 in cell 33 Fresnes prison; she had been for many months in solitary confinement in that prison and when she came to live with me her health was seriously impaired by this inhuman procedure so dear to the Nazis, her weakness was extreme, she could no longer even eat the filthy repugnant food which was given to us.[10]

On 13 May 1944, Sansom was taken from her cell and transported to Avenue Foch. Travelling with her were fellow SOE agents Andrée Borrel, Diana Rowden, Vera Leigh, Yolande Beekman, Eliane Plewman and Madeleine Damerment, as well as Sonia Olschanezky, a German Jew who had been recruited in France to work for the JUGGLER circuit. This was Sansom's first opportunity to meet her fellow agents. All of the women had trained at different times and had gone into France separately. The other women had had the opportunity to meet and communicate with each other at Fresnes prison, but Sansom, who had been kept in solitary confinement, had been denied much of this contact. She had, however, seen Diana Rowden during her time at Fresnes. Rowden had earned Sansom's eternal gratitude one afternoon in February when a group of prisoners had been transported to Rue des Saussaies for fingerprinting. Peter Churchill was in the group, and, as he and Sansom manoeuvred into position so that they could exchange a few words, Rowden had moved in front of them to block them from the view of the German sentry.

At Avenue Foch the women enjoyed a surprisingly comfortable day. Sansom requested that they be served tea, and the Germans complied. The women shared a lipstick that one of them had in their possession, and spent the day reminiscing and sharing their stories with each other. They talked about their mutual experiences at Avenue Foch, and took turns both encouraging and consoling each other.

Sansom was impressed by all of the women's bravery. Some of them cried, but Sansom felt optimistic. It was a beautiful spring day in Paris and she was finally in the company of other women. Things appeared much brighter than they had during her year-long confinement in Fresnes. Later that afternoon, the women were brought outside to be transported to the train station. Handcuffed together, the women were loaded aboard a train bound for Germany. Sansom was chained to Yolande Beekman, and they shared a compartment with Andrée Borrel and Vera Leigh. All of the women were apprehensive about their unknown destination. They had no idea whether they were being transported to another prison, a concentration camp, or their execution site. As the only one actually condemned to death at this point, Sansom was especially fearful.

The SOE agents were transported to Karlsruhe, a civil prison in Germany. Upon their arrival, the women were separated. Sansom was placed in a small dark cell with a German inmate, and life seemed better than it had at Fresnes. There was enough food to survive, she had the company of a cellmate, and prisoners could exercise in the prison yard and were expected to perform menial tasks, such as sewing or peeling potatoes, which helped to pass the time. She was even able to call greetings from her window when the SOE women were allowed out on the yard for separate exercise. At night, Sansom listened to the roar of the engines of the American and British bombers flying overhead, cautiously optimistic that end of the war was near, and praying that Allied bombs did not hit the prison. Then, without warning, Sansom was once again prepared for transport. This time her destination was Ravensbrück concentration camp.

By this time Sansom's health had been thoroughly compromised. A camp doctor told her she was likely suffering from tuberculosis, and offered to perform surgery on her lungs, but Sansom refused. Sansom was also suffering from both scurvy and dysentery. Her condition grew so grave that a camp guard actually told the camp Commandant, Fritz Suhren, that 'she would not live longer than a week if she were not cared for properly'.[11] Samson overheard this conversation, and thought that death would be a pleasure. Suhren had other plans, however. He began to visit Sansom in order to monitor her condition, and gave orders that she was to receive medical treatment for all of her conditions. He realised the potential value of having a relative of Winston Churchill as his prisoner, and was not prepared to lose her to disease or starvation. With no way to communicate with other prisoners, Sansom had no idea that the Allied armies were forcing a German retreat on all fronts. After the Allied forces had landed in Normandy in June 1944, they had slowly but steadily advanced against the German forces. The Russians in the east were also scoring victories against the Germans. By March 1945 the Americans had crossed the Rhine River into Germany, and by April the Russians had begun their assault on Berlin, the German capital. The Russians were also closing in on Ravensbrück. On 28 April 1944 a decision was made to vacate the camp, and hundreds of prisoners lost their lives during the evacuation. Some were executed to eliminate witnesses of the horrors of Ravensbrück, some were machine-gunned down while trying to escape, and some were simply too ill to survive the move. However, Sansom's deception with regard to her relationship to Winston Churchill saved her life. Fritz Suhren, recognising that the Germans were about to be overrun by the Russians, took Sansom as a hostage. Grabbed from her cell, Sansom was escorted out onto the exercise yard to wait while a car was brought for her. As she waited, she gazed around the camp, bewildered by its state of upheaval. Suddenly, a young girl of about eighteen or nineteen, head shaved but still relatively healthy-looking, was shot dead in front of her. The other female prisoners, driven crazy by hunger, descended up on the still-warm body, devouring it.

Shocked and horrified at what had just taken place, Sansom was grabbed and placed into the car with Suhren. Certain that this was the end, she assumed that she was being taken to a field or a wooded area, where she would be executed, leaving no trace. Suhren, though, had a different plan for Sansom. Hoping to trade his valuable hostage for his freedom, or at the very least preferential treatment, he drove with Sansom towards the American lines. After making contact with the Americans on 1 May 1945, Suhren handed Sansom over to an American officer. Sansom immediately told the American officers who Suhren was, and the horrors that he was responsible for, and the Americans took him into custody. Sansom refused the Americans' offer to find her a place to sleep for the night, choosing instead to spend the night in Suhren's car. It had been so long since she had seen the stars, she wanted to spend the night simply staring skyward. She also knew that Suhren had numerous documents in the car, and she was determined to read them and bring them back to Britain. The Americans arranged medical treatment for Sansom, who was in a deplorable physical state. When she was well enough to travel, she returned to Britain, arriving home on 8 May 1944. Fritz Suhren managed to escape custody but was arrested by the German police in 1949. In 1950 he was found guilty of war crimes and hanged.

Upon returning to Britain, Sansom continued to work for SOE, providing details about what had happened during her incarceration, which assisted in war crimes trials, and helping Vera Atkins track down what had happened to the other female agents who had never returned from France. She was also reunited with Peter Churchill, who like Samson had also survived the horrors of concentration camp life. Sansom decided her marriage to Roy was over, and the union was dissolved in 1946. She married Churchill in 1947. This marriage lasted until 1956, when Churchill sued for divorce on the grounds of adultery, and she married yet another former SOE agent, Geoffrey Hallowes, in 1957. A few years younger than Sansom, Hallowes was a very wealthy man and shared many common interests with her. She described him as a 'truly marvellous husband', and the two enjoyed a very happy life together.[12] Sansom was made a Member of the British Empire (MBE) in 1945, receiving the George Cross in 1946 and the Légion d'honneur in 1950 for the bravery she showed during her time as a German prisoner. There was some controversy regarding whether or not Sansom actually deserved these honours. After all, the torture she received and the interrogations where she allegedly revealed nothing were all conducted with few witnesses. However, extensive documentation of the torture she had received while incarcerated was provided by numerous medical experts, and Francis Cammaerts (code-named Roger) issued a certified statement indicating that Sansom alone knew the whereabouts of both he and the wireless operator Arnaud. The Germans were aware that she possessed this knowledge, and tortured Sansom to force her to reveal Roger and Arnaud's whereabouts. Since both Roger and Arnaud were able to continue their work unmolested, it was clear that Sansom had suffered in silence to protect her fellow agents.

Plagued by constant pain as a result of her wartime experiences, Sansom was declared permanently disabled, and was awarded the sum of £1,300 for her internment in Ravensbrück and a disability pension of £413 per year for the remainder of her life. She became heavily involved in numerous organisations, charities and causes, such as the National Poliomyelitis Association and Amnesty International, and even became Vice-President of the FANY in 1967. In 1993, at the age of eighty-one and despite being quite frail, she travelled to Ravensbrück to unveil a memorial plaque that had been crafted to honour the agents who had died at the camp.

Sansom's incredible self-sacrifice and determination earned her the admiration of her adopted country, Britain. Perhaps this was most clearly illustrated when Sansom's medals were stolen from her mother's home, and her mother, describing the sacrifice that had earned Sansom these honours, appealed through the press for their return. The thief, obviously a man with a conscience, returned the medals through the post, enclosing the following letter:

Your appeal for the return of the medals and orders of your very brave Odette and Captain Peter Churchill doesn't go in vain. You, madame, appear to be a dear, old lady. God bless you and your children. Thank you for having faith in me. I'm

Mathilde Carré (1910–70)
Code Name: The Cat/Victoire

While the female agents of the Second World War may have differed in many ways – including nationality, appearance, age, social background and assignment – their exploits commanded the respect of their peers and the gratitude of the country for which they served. Defiant in the face of danger, unwilling to yield even in the face of horrific torture, these women were ready to lay down their lives for their country. Such names as Szabo, Khan and Sansom, among many others, are spoken with reverence and respect. One agent's name, however, elicits a much less complimentary reaction. That agent is Mathilde Carré.

Most sources cite Mathilde's birthdate as 19 February 1910. Mathilde herself said she was born on 30 June 1908, in Le Creusot, France. Her given name was Mathilde-Lucie Bélard, and as a child she was always referred to as Lily. Shortly after her birth, Mathilde was turned over to her maternal grandfather and two spinster aunts to be raised, as her parents were far too busy enjoying one another, and keeping a busy social schedule, to raise a little girl. She saw her parents only sporadically, and was kept relatively isolated from other children. Her grandfather was quite wealthy, and she spent her early years in a vast house surrounded by splendid gardens, where her solitude helped to foster her vivid imagination. The onset of the First World War had little impact on young Mathilde. In 1914 her engineer father became a lieutenant and then a captain in the French army, and her mother spent most of the war following her husband to his various postings. Mathilde joined them both at Versailles when her father was sent there for a three-month mining course, but her contact with her parents remained limited. When she turned twelve, Mathilde left her grandfather's home and was enrolled in a private school in Orleans. Deprived of the companionship of her peers for so long, Mathilde revelled in her newfound social circle, and immediately set about making up for lost time. She discovered boys, and began 'to receive and then to write little love notes and to exchange kisses and rendezvous carefully arranged in advance'.[1] Despite her newfound social life, Mathilde was a capable student and did well in her first year in Orleans. However, during her second year a more unsavoury streak in her character began to manifest itself. Mathilde described herself as 'deceitful, untruthful and vicious', and she paid little heed to her schoolwork.[2] She wished only to do what she wanted, and viewed school as a tedious irritation. Upon being demoted to a lower grade, Mathilde's keen sense of self-preservation kicked in. Following a reprimand by the headmistress, Mathilde threw herself down a flight of stairs. For this, Mathilde received an outpouring of care and concern, and there was no further mention of her poor attitude towards academics. When recounting the incident, Mathilde noted smugly, 'I had won.'[3] Mathilde had discovered that by manipulating people she was often able to obtain what she wanted. Longing for teacher. For six years the marriage seemed to work well, but Carré was frustrated that the couple seemed unable to have children, and she was bored with life in North Africa. Aware that her marriage was foundering, Carré searched for a way out. A revelation from her mother-in-law provided her with just such an opportunity. Carré was shocked to learn that Maurice's father had died in a lunatic asylum, and that Maurice had suffered mumps as a child, rendering him sterile. Horrified by the thought of being married to a man who had a family history of insanity, and furious that Maurice had not told her about his inability to have children, Carré decided to leave her husband. The war in Europe had begun, and Maurice joined the army and was sent to Syria. Carré bid him goodbye and returned to France.

Upon returning to France, Carré immediately volunteered to work as a nurse for the French Red Cross. In April 1940, she was posted to a front-line hospital near the Maginot Line, which was a series of defensive fortifications and tank obstacles that the French had constructed, following the First World War, along their border with Germany. As the Germans smashed through Belgium and into France, the field hospitals became flooded with military and civilian casualties. Carré demonstrated great care for her patients and was untiring in her work. The French armies pulled back under the German onslaught and Carré was transferred to a hospital in Beauvais, just north of Paris. Once again Carré performed well under incredibly trying circumstances, and even received a military citation for her fine work. The French army was on the run, and soon so was Carré. Evacuation after evacuation took place as the hospital units were forced to pull back. Amid the nightly bombings,

He had been an Intelligence Officer in the Polish army, and after the collapse of Poland, in September 1939, he had joined the French to continue the fight against the Germans. Like Carré, Czerniawski had also made his way to the unoccupied zone after the fall of France. Czerniawski was determined to use his intelligence background to create a large espionage network, funded by London, which would operate out of Paris and send vital information to the British. After several weeks, he shared his plan with Carré, who was only too happy to join her new friend (and lover) in such an exciting enterprise. Carré travelled to Vichy, the capital city of the unoccupied zone, where she received instruction in espionage techniques from several officers who had served in the French Intelligence Bureau before the fall of France. She was taught basic espionage, including recruitment of agents, methods of coding, and the delivery and dissemination of information. Carré lodged at the Hôtel des Ambassadeurs, where her habit of scratching at the hotel's leather chairs earned her the nickname 'The Cat' (La Chatte) from some American reporters who were staying there. Czerniawski liked the name, and Carré adopted it as her code name.

Upon completing her training in Vichy, Carré planned to return to Paris, where she and Czerniawski would share a flat and could begin their intelligence-gathering work. Yet before she could leave, her husband Maurice showed up, begging her to return to North Africa with him. Carré had no intention of going with Maurice, but in an effort to avoid a scene she told him she would go to Paris to collect her things, and would return and meet up with him so that they could travel to Algiers together. She never did return, so Maurice left for Algiers alone. He was eventually killed during the Allied invasion of Italy, never having seen Carré again. Carré and Czerniawski, meanwhile, established themselves in Paris. They made numerous contacts and recruited a number of influential Frenchmen to assist them in their intelligence-gathering endeavours. Their organisation was called Interallié. After obtaining a short-wave radio, they were able to establish contact with their recruits in a number of French cities. Carré worked as both a recruiter and a courier. Both she and Czerniawski were responsible for receiving all of the agents' reports, verifying them and collating them into one larger weekly report that was sent to London. The extensive nature of the reports they received revealed how well organised the Interallié was. They had agents reporting the strength of the land forces in each French sector, the location of fuel dumps and power stations, the number of ships seen in certain harbours on any given day, pill box locations, invasion exercises, the number of genuine and dummy aircraft at given airfields and numerous other vital bits of intelligence. Carré herself would often gather information by flirting with German officers in the Paris cafés. She cultivated their attentions and they often let vital bits of information slip out during their conversations with her. Her café flirtations put Carré at great personal risk. Not only was she making herself known to the enemy, but she also risked being labelled as a '*collaborateur*' and being assaulted by the French civilians, who might view her flirtations with the Germans as treason! Aside from the use of her feminine wiles, Carré was quite imaginative in her intelligence-gathering schemes. On one occasion, after noticing a For Sale sign in a small café located just opposite Orly airport, Carré approached the owner as a potential buyer and asked permission for her architectural advisor to make some sketches of the property for possible alterations. The 'architectural advisor' then proceeded to document the types of planes at the airport, as well as the locations of the hangars and anti-aircraft installations, while Carré conversed with the café owner. Carré and Czerniawski also combed the daily newspapers, searching for news items describing the political situation in France as well as propaganda items that might interest the British. Every Wednesday, Carré carried their full written military report to the Gare de Lyon (train station) where she handed it to another agent (an example of a 'live' letter drop). This agent would board the train to Marseille and then proceed to conceal the message underneath the plaque located above the train's lavatory (an example of a 'dead' letter drop). An agent from Marseille would collect the report and forward it on to both Vichy and London.

The Interallié was extremely successful in its work. So successful, in fact, that the Germans realised that there was a highly organised and efficient Resistance circuit operating right underneath their noses. The Germans became increasingly vigilant, and radio-detection finders combed the streets of Paris. Suspicious persons were often arrested at railway stations or simply grabbed off the street. It was becoming more and more dangerous to be involved in undercover work. Carré soon discovered this on one of her recruiting and surveillance trips to the French coast. She had been sent to the French port of Brest, both to recruit fishermen for service in Interallié, and to review and report back on the damage done by a recent British air raid. Knowing that the citizens of Brest were largely pro-British in their sentiments, Carré decided to gain their confidence by pretending to be an Englishwoman. She spoke to the citizens using a thick British accent, and in doing so attracted the attention of an undercover Gestapo (German police) agent. He followed her on the train back to Paris and approached her as she was eating breakfast in a café. Engaging her in conversation the agent was quite shocked to discover that Mathilde spoke with a perfect French accent. When he revealed that he was a Gestapo inspector and that he had followed her because of her use of an English accent, Carré was terrified. The inspector demanded to know why she had visited Brest. Carré had to think fast. Deciding it was best to play the part of a silly and frivolous woman, she replied, 'There has been so much talk about the RAF raids that, as an inquisitive woman with plenty of time on her hands, I wanted to see it for myself. To amuse myself I put on an English accent to find out the reactions of the townspeople.'[4] The Gestapo inspector simply shook his head and laughed, satisfied that Carré was nothing more than a bored housewife.

By October 1941 the increase of German activity in their neighbourhood forced Carré and Czerniawski to move to another part of Paris. Czerniawski travelled to London where he met with Special Operations Executive (SOE) officers, and was told that SOE would soon be dropping its own agents into France to assist Interallié with its espionage and sabotage objectives. This was great news for Interallié, and there was little reason for the group not to be optimistic about the continued success of their network. However, after Czerniawski returned from London, two things happened that would ultimately have devastating results for both

Interallié and Mathilde Carré. First, Czerniawski brought a woman named Renée Borni into the group. Her code name was Violette, and she was given the job of decoding radio messages. She also served as Czerniawski's mistress, and was extremely jealous of Carré. Carré, who had also been romantically involved with Czerniawski, loathed her new rival. Secondly, one of Interallié's agents was arrested by the Gestapo in Cherbourg. The agent's name was Raul Kiffer (code name Kiki), and he was apprehended by an Abwehr sergeant by the name of Hugo Bleicher. Bleicher was a patient and skilled interrogator, and he convinced Kiffer that Interallié was on the verge of collapse and that the only way he could avoid being handed over to the Gestapo was to cooperate with Bleicher. Kiffer was used to contact a second Interallié agent, who revealed the address of the group's headquarters. With Hugo Bleicher hot on the trail, Interallié's days were numbered.

On 17 November 1941, Bleicher and the German police burst through the door of Czerniawski's apartment. Both he and Renée Borni (Violette) were taken into custody. Czerniawski refused to talk, but Borni was determined to save her own life. She offered to identify one of Interallié's most important agents, 'The Cat', for Bleicher. Bleicher encouraged Borni to tell him everything she knew, and he kept her with him as he organised surveillance of the apartment. The pair watched and waited. Carré, who had spent the night at her friend Mirielle's home, headed back to Czerniawski's apartment early the next morning. Although she was warned that German police had been sighted in the neighbourhood, Carré was determined to return to the apartment to collect some of her personal items. As she neared the apartment, she noticed that there was quite a bit of activity on the street, which was unusual for that time of the morning. Carré was approached by the German police and asked to show her identity card. When it was returned to her, she continued up the street, careful to not look at Czerniawski's apartment. Carré sensed she was being followed. She paused outside a print shop and pretended to look at the window display. Here she was approached by another policeman, and questioned as to why she was out on the streets so early in the morning. Carré quickly concocted a story that she was out shopping for prints, but the shop was closed. She declined the policeman's invitation to lunch, and retraced her route back from where she had come. Passing by Czerniawski's apartment for the second time, she glanced quickly at it and saw that the front door had been broken in. A German officer came out of the doorway and arrested Carré on the spot. As she was led away, Carré was shocked to see a familiar face standing with what was obviously a German officer. Recalling the incident, Carré stated flatly, 'I saw Violette on the pavement with a man in mufti ... He was obviously asking her if I was The Cat for she nodded her head.'[5] Carré spent the night in a cold, damp cell in the women's prison of La Santé. Early the next morning she was taken into Paris for interrogation, and formally introduced to Hugo Bleicher. Bleicher informed her that the Germans expected Carré to work for them, and that if she wanted to live she would agree to this arrangement. He even went so far as to promise her freedom by the end of the day! Having confiscated her diary, Bleicher knew that Carré was supposed to meet with one of Interallié's agents later that morning. Bleicher escorted Mathilde to the rendezvous point, and when the unfortunate agent approached Carré he was arrested. From there Bleicher and Carré travelled to her friend Mirielle's home to collect all of the Interallié money that had been in Carré's possession. Both Mirielle and her husband were arrested. After this Bleicher forced Carré to call her uncle, who was also involved in Interallié, to arrange a meeting with him and another Interallié agent, her childhood friend René Aubertin. Carré complied, and both her uncle and Aubertin were apprehended. Incredibly, at the end of this horrific day Carré asked about Bleicher's promise to free her! Bleicher's response was that she was now free but that it was too dangerous for her to be released because of the possible backlash against her for her role in the day's arrests. He explained that she was in his protective custody and that he would take good care of her. That evening, the two became lovers.

Bleicher continued to use Carré as a decoy so that he could arrest the agents of the Interallié. Carré would arrange a meeting with a certain agent, and at the meeting Bleicher would make the arrest. The system worked well, since once the arrest was made the agent could not inform anyone else of Carré's duplicity. Bleicher also recovered one of Interallié's radio transmitters, which he used with devastating results. He had Carré write a message to London indicating that Czerniawski and Renée Borni had been captured, but that she was willing to take control of Interallié and continue to run the network. Carré composed hundreds of messages to London, each containing misinformation planted by the Germans, while another captured wireless operator transmitted them. Much to Carré's chagrin, Renée Borni was brought in to code the messages. The two women continued to detest one another and Carré, rather understandably, could not forgive Borni for betraying her to the Germans. Changing her code name from 'The Cat' to 'Victoire', Carré was completely successful in duping the British. The proof came when Carré sent a request for money so that she could pay her agents. London directed her to an apartment house in Paris where she collected the money. Clearly she had gained London's trust. Perhaps her most successful ploy against the British involved the German ships the *Prinz Eugen*, the *Scharnhorst*, and the *Gneisenau*. The Germans were having difficulty getting these warships out of Brest harbour, as the Royal Navy lay in wait just outside, ready to pounce. While the British were successful in keeping the German ships bottled up, their own ships were vulnerable to German air attack, and the Royal Navy desperately wanted to put these ships to work elsewhere. The Royal Air Force (RAF) attacked the German ships in Brest harbour, hoping to damage them so badly that there would be no risk of the Germans sending them into the open sea. Virtually no damage was done to the German ships by the RAF bombs, but Carré sent numerous messages to the British that the ships were badly damaged and out of commission. The British believed Carré's reports, and relaxed their vigil on Brest harbour, removing most of the ships from the blockade. On the evening of 11 February 1942, the German warships broke out of Brest and reached the open sea, free to prey on Allied shipping.

Well fed, elegantly housed and fawned over by her solicitous new German friends, Carré may have felts pangs of remorse about what she was doing but she was undeniably comfortable in her new situation. She always tried to make the best of the opportunities that were presented to her. However, she was not a stupid woman, and she knew that if Bleicher ever tired of her, or if the Germans no longer found her useful, she could easily find herself quickly dispatched to a concentration camp. Her sense of self-preservation was keenly honed and she was always 'on the lookout' for ways in which to ensure both her comfort and safety. In 1942 yet another opportunity would present itself, and she would prove, once again, to be adaptable.

Pierre de Vomécourt, an SOE agent who had been dropped into France during May 1941, was desperate to make contact with London. His network of undercover operatives had been infiltrated, and many members of his group were arrested. The arrest of his wireless operator was a crushing blow, leaving de Vomécourt with no means of contacting London. De Vomécourt's mission had been to observe whether support for the French Resistance movement was strong enough to warrant the British sending in drops of materials such as arms and ammunition. At that time, Britain was still trying to recover from the loss of materials they had suffered at Dunkirk, and could little afford to be sending supplies into France if the Resistance was in no position to put them to good use. De Vomécourt had discovered the Resistance movement was alive and well, and knew he needed to inform his superiors in London that the Resistance was desperate for British supplies. Tentatively, de Vomécourt began putting out feelers, hoping to find another Resistance group whose wireless operator could transmit his messages back to SOE. A friend of de Vomécourt, Michel Brault, was familiar with the Interallié network and offered to put de Vomécourt in touch with Mathilde Carré. Unfortunately, that, if she fell from Bleicher's favour, she could be packed off to a concentration camp. Moreover, de Vomécourt was becoming suspicious of Carré. A series of troubling events had occurred, including the arrests and attempted arrests of several individuals who had had contact with Mathilde. There was also a telegram that Carré had delivered late to de Vomécourt, which caused him to miss a rendezvous with an SOE aircraft. Michel Brault was surprised to discover that Carré had in her possession a photograph, which had only recently been taken to create a forged passport, of an important Resistance figure, Colonel François Michel. Brault began to theorise that perhaps the colonel had been arrested, and somehow his passport photograph had been given to Carré by the Germans. Within days of Brault's discovery of the photograph, an attempt was made to arrest him and he found himself on the run. He met with de Vomécourt to describe what had happened, and the two men speculated about who could have denounced Brault. Carré's name was mentioned as a possibility. De Vomécourt informed Carré about the attempt to arrest Brault, and she offered to procure some forged papers so that Brault could cross into the relative safety of Vichy France. After a few days, Carré produced some fake identity papers that looked incredibly genuine. De Vomécourt began to wonder just how good Carré's German contacts were, and he confronted her with his suspicions about her loyalties. Carré, worried about how much longer Bleicher would find her useful, decided to reveal to de Vomécourt that she was working for the Germans, and offered to begin working for the British once again.

De Vomécourt was not entirely shocked by Carré's admission, for he trusted no one wholeheartedly. However, he was in an extremely difficult position. He could have killed Carré for her admission, but that would have brought down the wrath of the Germans upon his group. If he refused to work with her, she could simply tell the Germans that de Vomécourt was on to them, and once again his group would suffer the consequences. De Vomécourt decided that his safest course of action would be to use Carré as a triple agent, and after the war he described her reaction to his plan to author Gordon Young, stating, 'When I told her how we could hoodwink the Germans and counter-infiltrate them, I felt at once that it was the kind of game she understood and loved to play. And well she played it. As I knew her then, she was clever, ruthless and totally self-centred.'[6]

He agreed with her suggestion that she work as a triple agent against the Germans, and even proposed that she accompany him to Britain so that she could describe the inner workings of German counter-intelligence to SOE. As further 'bait' to encourage the Germans to allow de Vomécourt and Carré to depart for England, de Vomécourt had Carré tell the Germans that he would be bringing back an officer, possibly of the General rank, to take control of the various Resistance factions in an effort to maintain order and reduce friction among the groups. Hugo Bleicher was extremely excited at the thought of being able to arrest a British general and, obviously secure in the belief that Carré was loyal to him, agreed to let her go! Bleicher even stated, 'I will pay the penalty if she betrays me. I know her intimately and I know that she cannot betray us.'[7] Carré was instructed to find out the names of all of the agents working in France, and then to return with de Vomécourt. De Vomécourt was still unsure if he could trust Carré and before they left for

Britain he put a safety plan in place. Should Mathilde betray him, his brother Philippe de Vomécourt had instructions to kill her. Philippe also sent a message to SOE through a neutral embassy in Vichy that Carré's radio was controlled by the Germans. De Vomécourt and Carré's departure date was set for February, and after several failed attempts to leave France they were finally picked up by a British torpedo boat on the evening of 26 February 1942. As the pair boarded the boat, the Germans watched from a distance, carefully documenting the procedure the British used for extracting their agents out of France. In fact, German coastguard boats and ground patrols had been warned to steer clear of the embarkation point so that Carré and de Vomécourt were guaranteed a safe departure.

After arriving in Dartmouth harbour, de Vomécourt made it very clear to SOE that Carré's loyalties were suspect, described to them what he knew about her work for the Germans and explained how he had turned her into a triple agent. The British decided to let Carré believe that they viewed her as a trusted agent, and assigned her a beautiful flat at Porchester Gate overlooking Hyde Park. Carré was completely unaware that the flat was riddled with hidden microphones. She was interrogated about her role in the German counter-intelligence service but, aside from being closely watched, she lived the next few months in relative freedom. Carré had no idea she was the topic of several meetings between MI5 (the domestic branch of British Military Intelligence), SIS (Secret Intelligence Service, the foreign branch of British Military Intelligence), SOE and Polish Intelligence regarding whether or not she could be trusted. She visited tourist attractions, cafés and shops, all

There is no evidence that an affair actually took place between Selborne and Carré, and, indeed, it would have been quite difficult considering how closely Mathilde was watched. However, the concerns voiced by Mrs Barton certainly attest to the power Carré felt she was able to exercise over men!

Carré talked to her British interviewers extensively about German counter-intelligence, describing to the British a German radio code and German methods of arrest and interrogation. She also gave them insights into the morale of the French population. At no point during her time of freedom in Britain did SOE ever discover even a hint of proof that she was still working for the Germans, so it would appear that she had, in fact, returned her loyalties to the British. Carré truly believed that the British considered her a valuable and important player in the world of espionage, and was shocked, therefore, when she was arrested on 1 July 1942 and incarcerated at Holloway prison. SOE had been busy the past few months, investigating a variety of reports that had trickled in describing the extent of Carré's treachery and the number of people whose lives she had put in jeopardy. Moreover, de Vomécourt had gone back to France in April and was arrested a short time after he landed. Since de Vomécourt was supposed to return to France with Carré, the British were fairly certain the Germans would be alerted to the fact that Carré was now under British control. Once SOE was sure that Carré had provided them as much information about the Germans as she could, the order was sent down for her arrest. Carré was a dreadful prisoner, constantly refusing to cooperate, insulting the prison matrons, and frequently denouncing SOE and threatening to kill 'F' Section Chief, Colonel Buckmaster. After a year at Holloway, in June 1943

Carré was transferred to Aylesbury prison where she spent the remainder of the war. Her rage seemed to diminish and it was here that she began writing her memoirs.

On 1 June 1945 Carré, accompanied by two Scotland Yard detectives, travelled by ferry across the English Channel back to France where she was kept in prison for over three years until she was brought to trial. Charged with treason for her work with German counter-intelligence, witness after witness was brought forward to describe The Cat's treachery. The witnesses included René Aubertin, who had survived Mauthausen concentration camp and was able to describe the horrific death by beating (by camp guards) of another agent who had been denounced by Carré. Mathilde's old friend Mirielle, who along with her husband had been arrested as a result of Carré's duplicity, took the witness stand and explained that she was now a widow, since her husband had perished during his incarceration at Mauthausen. Combined with the testimony against her, Carré's own personality did little to help her cause. During the trial she was often hostile and defiant, and did little to endear herself to those judging her. Statements she made, such as 'I only denounced the more stupid ones' and 'There had to be victims ... I had sometimes to sacrifice men ... this is just the fortune of war', created the impression that she was a woman without remorse.[10] Carré was found guilty of treason, and condemned to death. Thanks to a vigorous plea for mercy on the part of her defence attorney, who asked that the court consider the valuable work Carré had done for the Resistance before her arrest, her death sentence was commuted to life imprisonment. Her sentence was further commuted a few years later, and in 1954 Carré was released from prison. She lived with her parents in Paris for a while, before moving to an undisclosed location in the country. In 1959 she re-emerged briefly to publish her memoirs, entitled *J'ai Été 'La Chatte'* (*I Was 'The Cat'*). Carré's years in prison had taken their toll, and she was now a middle-aged matron with failing eyesight. Mathilde Carré lived the remainder of her life in seclusion, and she died in 1970.

city, and Krystyna enjoyed a privileged childhood with her father, Count Jerzy Skarbek, and her wealthy Jewish mother, Stefania. The Skarbek marriage was not a happy one, with the count engaging in numerous infidelities, but he doted on his young daughter, calling her his 'Star'. The count encouraged Krystyna's tomboyish nature, and by his side she became an expert skier and horsewoman. Krystyna is remembered as an energetic and happy child, with a definite wild streak. Her mother, as well as the mothers of the other little girls in her social circle, was dismayed by Krystyna's high-spirited nature, but her father found her amusing. Her difficulties conforming to authority were strongly evident when she was sent to be educated at the Sacré-Coeur convent school in western Poland. Unhappy about being separated from her father and her relatively 'free' existence on the family estates, Krystyna defied all of the convent's rules and regulations, even going so far as to set fire to a priest's robes during Mass. She was eventually asked to leave Sacré-Coeur and was sent to a stricter convent school. While Krystyna was away at school her family suffered a serious financial blow that forced them to sell many of their landholdings, including the family estate. Her family's difficulties had a sobering effect on Krystyna and she decided that, instead of adding to her family's problems, she would do everything she could to succeed at her new school. She was soon at the top of her class, and is remembered as an incredibly popular student. Higher education was not in the cards for Krystyna, however. Her father died of tuberculosis in 1930 and there was little money left to support the family. Krystyna was forced to go to work and she eventually took a position in a Fiat car agency. Although the agency was a great place for meeting wealthy young men, Krystyna, with her adventurous spirit and aristocratic background, found clerical work both tiresome and beneath her. To make matters worse, her office was located above the garage, and the petrol fumes floating up through the floor left damaging scars on her lungs. Little did she know that those scars would later prove useful during her work as an undercover agent.

With a bubbly personality and striking good looks (she did not win the Miss Poland title as many writers claim, but she was one of the runners-up in the 1930 Miss Polonia contest), she attracted many male admirers. One of them was businessman Gustav Gettlich, whom Krystyna met at the Fiat agency. Advised by her doctors that exposure to mountain air might help to treat her damaged lungs, Krystyna spent a great deal of time in the upscale skiing town of Zakopane in the Carpathian Mountains, and Gettlich became her constant companion. They married in April 1930 when Krystyna was twenty-two, but, although he offered both Krystyna and her family financial security, the pair soon recognised that they were incompatible, and the marriage was dissolved without malice. Some ill feelings must have existed, however, for years later, when asked to describe his first wife, Gettlich declined to sing her praises, stating simply that Krystyna was 'dotty, romantic and forever craving change'.[1] Free again, and with an ample settlement from Gettlich to support her in comfort, Krystyna became a well-known figure on Warsaw's social circuit, captivating most who met her and engaging in many flirtations. She also spent much of her time skiing and travelling, and, in her spare time, engaged in smuggling black market goods through the mountains of the Polish frontier. Her smuggling activities seemed to feed her thirst for excitement, and her familiarity with this territory later served her very well in her capacity as a secret agent, when she needed to travel covertly in and out of Occupied Poland.

In 1938 she met Jerzy Giżycki, a wealthy man who already had links with the British Secret Service. He had returned to Zakopane from an adventurous life abroad to enjoy the beauty of the mountains, along with skiing, hiking and the town's lively social scene. It was here that he connected with Krystyna, whom he described in his memoirs as an 'excellent horse-woman, fair skier, and the most intrepid human being I have ever met – man or woman'.[2] Despite a considerable age difference (Giżycki was nearly fifty), the two were married in November 1938. Giżycki was an adventurer with a passion for Africa, and both he and Krystyna were living there when the Germans invaded Poland in September 1939. Shocked by the speed and brutality of the German assault on their homeland, and stirred by a deep sense of patriotism (mingled with, perhaps, a thirst for adventure), the couple left immediately for Great Britain, arriving in October 1939. They both offered their services to the Secret Intelligence Service (MI6). A notation in Krystyna's personnel file, dated 7 December 1939, reads, 'She is a very smart looking girl, simply dressed and aristocratic. She is a flaming Polish patriot ... an expert skier and a great adventuress ... She is absolutely fearless herself and certainly makes that impression.'[3]

The British were extremely interested in using Krystyna. Desperate to establish reliable intelligence about what exactly was happening in Occupied Poland, as well as to let the operations. Kowerski focused on helping interned Polish soldiers escape Occupied Poland, while Krystyna's missions focused more on intelligence gathering and courier work than on her original assignment as a propagandist. Krystyna made several trips across the mountains into Poland. The first was during February 1940, when she and two others made the perilous trek across the mountains into Polish territory. They risked both German patrols and blizzards, but eventually made it to Zakopane, where Krystyna rested a few days before travelling on to Warsaw. Once in the capital, she spent several weeks gathering information and establishing contacts among the Polish population. Granville was shocked at the Germans' brutal treatment of the Poles, and was well aware how dangerous her mission was. She made contact with the underground Polish press and gave them the British propaganda material to reproduce and distribute. Krystyna also made some assessments of her own, reporting to the British that their propaganda leaflet droppings were well received by the Poles, but correctly assuming that the population might appreciate news of the war instead. She recommended that British and Allied news reports be broadcast at fixed times and on fixed wavelengths so that regular Polish radio sets could pick them up. By connecting with numerous local resistance groups Krystyna collected a wealth of information for the British, including details about German troop transports heading towards Russia or Turkey and Romania, the distribution of military units throughout the country, existing industrial capacity in Poland, and how German supplies were being transported throughout the region. Armed with this intelligence, Krystyna caught a train to the mountains, leaping from her car as the train slowed upon its approach to the station. From there she hiked cross-country for several days through Slovakia before finally arriving at the Hungarian border and making her way back to Budapest.

In October 1940 a courier arrived from Poland with information that some British airmen were hiding in Warsaw and needed to find passage back to Britain. Krystyna offered to guide the men out, and set off in November, taking a route through Ukraine with a partner, Father Laski. By the time they reached Warsaw, they discovered that the Polish Underground had already sent the airmen out through a Russian escape route, where most of the men had been captured and turned over to the Germans. Two managed to make it back to Warsaw, and Father Laski escorted them back to Budapest. Krystyna remained behind to make inquiries about her family. She finally tracked down her mother, and pleaded with her to leave the country. The Germans' anti-Jewish measures were becoming more and more oppressive. Jewish property was being confiscated, and Jews were being rounded up and placed in ghettos or forcibly deported to work camps. Krystyna recognised the danger, but Stefania did not. Having converted to Catholicism, Stefania had never registered as a Jew and was in fact living, illegally, outside of the Jewish ghetto. Krystyna made plans with friends to hide her mother in an isolated forest cabin until arrangements could be made to transport her out of Poland, but Stefania refused to leave Warsaw. Frustrated by her mother's obstinacy, Krystyna had no choice but to leave Poland without her. The Countess Skarbek was arrested by the Gestapo shortly after Krystyna's second visit, and Krystyna never saw her mother again.

Krystyna's work during this period was extremely important. She passed on valuable bits of intelligence to the British, and established an escape line for both Poles (seeking to escape the harshness of German occupation, or conscription into forced-labour camps) and prisoners of war (POWs) to slip out of Poland. In fact, two British prisoners who were taken captive at Dunkirk used Krystyna's escape line, and were the first POWs to make it back to Great Britain. Krystyna was arrested twice during the time she worked out of Budapest. The first time she was stopped by border guards as she was trying to cross back into Poland. She managed to destroy the incriminating documents she was carrying by flinging them into a river, and convinced the guards that they would be better off simply taking the large sum of money she had in her possession for themselves than handing both her and the money over to the Germans. Her second arrest came in January 1941. Krystyna and Andrzej's work smuggling both Polish and British prisoners out of Poland, and their intelligence-gathering activities (which provided the British with detailed information regarding the position of ammunition and aircraft factories in Poland), had attracted the attention of both Hungarian and German authorities. On 24 January 1941 they were arrested by the Hungarian police and turned over to the Gestapo for questioning. Interrogated separately, the lovers steadfastly denied working for the British. Krystyna proceeded to bite down hard upon her tongue, causing bleeding. She feigned a coughing fit as well, causing immediate concern among her captors that their prisoner was in the advanced stages of tuberculosis. An X-ray of her lungs revealed the scarring she had suffered as a result of the gas fumes from the Fiat

Granville had been working with and the pair themselves to be suspicious. All support of Granville's organisation was withdrawn, and a memo dated 20 January 1942 indicates that the British viewed both Granville and Kennedy as potential sources of danger. The Polish government in exile, which was formed after the German and Soviet occupation of Poland in 1939 and based in London, also resented the fact that Granville was working for the British. The government in exile commanded all Polish forces operating in Poland and abroad, and the British government had promised the Poles that all communications with Poland would be done through official Polish channels. Granville had reported directly to the British, and many in the exiled Polish government felt that this violated the promise Britain had made to them. There also was concern about sending the pair back into the field since their well-known reputations, Granville's stunning physical appearance and Kennedy's artificial leg made it difficult to conceal their identities. With all of these factors at play, both Granville and Kennedy spent most of 1941 and 1942 effectively sidelined from the war effort. However, by 1943 SOE was convinced of Granville and Kennedy's loyalty, and began actively training the pair with an eye towards using them as agents once again. Patrick Howarth, head of the Polish-Czech section of SOE in Cairo, was one of Granville's most ardent supporters and stated, after the war, that the most useful contribution he made to the war effort was reinstating Granville into active service. As with many female agents, Granville was assigned to the FANYs (First Aid Nursing Yeomanry), and senior FANY officer Gwendoline Lees was put in charge of briefing her. Lees was so deeply impressed with her charge that she named her first daughter after her. After the war Lees recounted that she felt Granville was one of the most remarkable women she'd ever known, and recalled both her deep love for Andrew Kennedy and her total dedication to the liberation of her Polish homeland. After her recruitment into the FANY, Granville was sent for training in the use of wireless transmitters, parachute jumping, demolition, preparation of reception committees and the creation of simple personal disguises. In early 1944, Kennedy was sent to Italy to act as an instructor at a parachuting school. In May 1944, the decision was made to drop Granville into France.

Francis Cammaerts was one of SOE's most distinguished agents. Code-named Roger, he headed up the Resistance network JOCKEY, which extended throughout south-eastern France. In September 1943, Cammaerts lost his courier, Cecily Lefort, when she was arrested by the Gestapo. The majority of French males had been conscripted into the German labour force and therefore could not roam about the countryside without raising suspicion. A female courier was vital to the continued success of Cammaerts' network. Brooks Richards, Head of SOE from 1943 to 1944 in Corsica and southern France, had met Granville and felt she was 'a most remarkable lady', and he was determined to have her fill the role as Cammaerts' courier.[4] Assigned the code name Pauline and the cover name·Jacqueline Armand, Granville parachuted into France on 8 July 1944. With her she took a loaded revolver, torch, identification documents, ration cards, money and an 'L' tablet – a cyanide pill that could kill instantly, should an arrested agent prefer death to torture.

Blown many miles off course, Granville had a rough entry into France. She landed badly, bruising her tail bone and damaging her revolver beyond repair. Since she disliked firing guns, the loss of the weapon didn't bother her, and she quickly buried her parachute and the damaged revolver before going in search of her reception committee. Granville soon linked up with Cammaerts and got immediately to work. She organised reception committees for the drops of arms, ammunition and supplies, and often accompanied the reception committees on their late-night missions. She then had to organise the unpacking and delivery of the dropped materials to the Resistance. Most of these activities took place during the evenings but Granville's days were full too. She worked tirelessly at her courier duties, taking messages to all members of Cammaerts' network as well as to the Resistance. Her first week in France was busy, but was about to become even more intense. The region in which Granville had been dropped was about to become the site of a major battle.

A large group of French Resistance fighters had declared the Vercors plateau liberated from German occupation. This declaration ignored the fact that the plateau was located well within German-occupied territory. The Vercors is a heavily forested and mountainous area covered with villages and farms. The French Resistance felt well protected in this area, as it was a natural fortress, and had amassed a large number of armed fighters. British planes had been dropping supplies into the Vercors since early June, but on 14 July 1944 hundreds of Allied planes flew overhead, dropping over a thousand containers of supplies into the region. Guns, ammunition, food, clothes and cigarettes were parachuted down, adorned with the message, 'Bravo lads. Vive la France.'[5] While the Resistance fighters were exhilarated by the drop, cheering and celebrating their windfall, Cammaerts was dismayed, as the drop had occurred in broad daylight in full view of the Germans. He knew the Germans would not stand idly by and allow the situation in the Vercors to continue unchecked, and his dismay was well founded. The German response to the presence of this large group of French Resistance fighters was immediate and brutal. Carpet-bombing and strafing of the plateau soon began. With superior manpower and weapons, the Germans bottled up the Vercors, guarding every land and water exit and entry. Villages were occupied and burned, and numerous civilians were tortured and executed. Panic began to spread through the region, and both Granville and Cammaerts sent numerous radio requests for help, pleading for more weapons and for the nearest German airfield to be bombed. Their requests went unanswered. Early in the morning of 20 July Granville was delivering a message for Cammaerts to a barn at the end of the Vassieux airstrip when hundreds of enemy gliders descended upon the field. Under a steady barrage of machine-gun fire, Granville managed to make her way down the hill at the back of the strip and report the German landing to Cammaerts. With the sense that all was lost, Granville and Cammaerts managed to escape through the last available exit route on 22 July 1944.

After this narrow escape, Granville resumed her courier duties for Cammaerts, as well as embarking on several missions of her own creation. Granville was convinced that she could incite large-scale desertions by foreigners (manpower from all German-occupied territory) who had been conscripted into the German army, and by the troops of German allies. By spreading the word that the Allied armies had the Germans on the run, many of the foreign conscripts saw an end to their subjugation and leapt at the opportunity to turn on their German oppressors. Similarly, soldiers from the Italian armies (German allies) proved eager to sever their ties with the Germans. Granville made contact with Russian, Italian and Polish army groups, and was extremely successful in convincing hundreds of soldiers either to desert or to join the Resistance. The influence of her personality extended to animals as well. One evening, as she was attempting to avoid a German patrol, Granville found herself seeking refuge under some brush in a roadside ditch. One of the Alsatian dogs from the patrol discovered her, but before the dog could sound the alarm Granville wrapped her arms around it and pulled it to her side. The Germans called for the dog, but he remained by Christine's side all night. The dog became devoted to Granville and remained with her until the Liberation. Granville had many close calls as she went about her work, and was caught by the Germans on more than one occasion. Each time, however, she managed to talk her way out of arrest by playing the part of a simple peasant girl who could not possibly have anything to hide. On one such occasion, though, she did have to resort to a threat of violence. Attempting to pass through the Alps with some Italian partisans, she and one of the Italians were discovered by a border patrol. With a grenade in each hand, Granville threatened to blow up the lot of them if the Germans did not let them go. Convinced of her sincerity, the border guards swiftly departed, and Granville and her companion slipped off into the underbrush.

(another SOE operative) and a French officer named Sorensen were travelling by car through the French countryside when they were stopped by a Gestapo roadblock. Fielding pretended not to know Cammaerts and Sorensen, claiming to be a hitchhiker. After a search of the men's pockets, however, the Germans discovered that each man was carrying a large sum of money and that all of the bills had consecutive serial numbers. They were identified as members of the Resistance, and immediately arrested and sent to Digne prison, where they sentenced to be shot. Upon hearing of their capture, Granville went to the local French Resistance group and suggested that she lead them in an attack on the prison. The Resistance fighters thought the risk was too great for the rescue of only three men, and refused to consider Granville's plan. Frustrated by the lack of Resistance support, and determined to rescue her colleagues, Granville decided to rely on guile and deception as opposed to brute force. She borrowed a bicycle and travelled to Digne where she spent the next several days working tirelessly to secure her friends' release. She made contact with the Gestapo, claiming to be both Cammaerts' wife and the niece of British General Montgomery. Granville also came right out and admitted that the men in custody were extremely important Allied agents, and then spun a clever tale about how the Allied armies were within a few kilometres of Digne prison, and how the German officers would be treated mercilessly if anything were to happen to Cammaerts, Fielding and Sorensen. This was quite convincing since the Allied armies had, in fact, just landed in southern France (but of course were nowhere near as close as Granville made out). Offering the Gestapo officer protection from the Resistance fighters, and promising to tell the Allied army commanders of the benevolence shown by the Gestapo commander, Granville bargained for the freedom of her friends. The Gestapo officer, Max Waem, agreed to help Granville, but demanded that the British protect him from the vengeance of the French population, and that he remain a free man. Several sources also indicate that Waem demanded 2 million francs for his assistance, and describe how Granville leapt on her bicycle and pedalled the 25-mile journey back to her safe house, where she instructed her wireless operator to signal Algiers that they required 2 million francs to secure the release of Cammaerts, Fielding and Sorensen. According to these sources, the SOE placed such a high regard on Cammaerts' life that the ransom was dropped by a Royal Air Force (RAF) plane that very evening. Brooks Richards confirmed the parachute drop in an interview he gave after the war. Curiously, however, neither Granville nor Cammaerts mentions the 2 million francs in their official statements with regard to this incident; nor does the timeline cited by Granville support this story. In Granville's official statement she indicates that her conversation with Waem lasted about three hours, during which time she convinced him to release the prisoners. They arranged to meet at a rendezvous point in an hour's time, and Waem subsequently arrived with Cammaerts, Fielding and Sorensen. Apparently Waem had returned to the prison and ordered the prisoners out of their cells, claiming that he was taking them for interrogation. He marched them to the prison gates, where, just outside and around the corner, Granville was waiting in a car. Fielding, Cammaerts and Sorensen left the prison mere hours before they were to have been executed. When referring to this feat in a letter recommending Granville for the George Cross (the United Kingdom's highest award for bravery and equal to the Victoria Cross), Major General W. Stawell wrote, 'The nerve, coolnss [*sic*], and devotion to duty and high courage of this lady which inspired and brought about a successful conclusion this astonishing coup de mains must certainly be considered as one of the most remarkable personal exploits of the war.'[6]

After securing the release of Cammaerts, Granville continued her work encouraging foreign conscripts in outlying German positions to abandon the war effort. She helped to maintain communication between the local Resistance fighters, who were working to make the German retreat as costly as possible. Granville also offered her services to the advancing American armies. On one occasion she was approached by an American captain, who was concerned about a potential German counter-attack in the area his troops had just taken. Discovering that the captain had a couple of thousand Polish prisoners (conscripts in the German army) in a makeshift POW camp nearby, and remembering her success with the Col de Larche garrison, Granville offered to see if the Poles would join the fight in support of the Americans. Addressing the prisoners in Polish, Granville explained the threat of a German counter-attack and asked for the Poles' help in defending against it. She also indicated that they would be required to fight naked to the waist, since they would not be allowed to fight in a German uniform and there were no extra American uniforms to be had. After listening to her impassioned speech, the soldiers removed their jackets and waved them enthusiastically in the air. Once again Granville had demonstrated her powers of persuasion.

By September, Paris had been liberated, and the Allied forces had swept across France and were advancing through Belgium and Holland. Granville's work as an operative in Occupied France gradually came to an end. She returned to Britain in November 1944, and a few weeks later was sent back to France where she was to launch a mission into Northern Italy. She crossed the frontier three times, establishing contacts between Britain and Italian resistance groups. These resistance groups provided a valuable service to the Allies by sabotaging communications between Italy and France as the Germans pulled back towards their homeland. Granville once again returned to Britain, where she enrolled in the Women's Auxiliary Air Force (WAAF) and was commissioned as a flight officer. However, as the war wound down, there was little opportunity for Granville to work in her chosen field. There was talk of sending her on a mission into Poland, but nothing came of it. The war in Europe ended in May 1945.

Granville and Kennedy were reunited after the war but discovered that they had grown apart. Despite a fondness for one another that would last their lifetimes, they were never again an exclusive couple. Neither one wanted to return to post-war Poland, which was now occupied by the Soviets, and they both searched for a place they could call home. Kennedy eventually found work in Germany, while Granville – who was awarded the George Medal in June 1945 (for saving the lives of two English officers, Cammaerts and Fielding); the French Croix de Guerre in November 1945 (for saving the life of Major Sorenson); and the Order of the British Empire in 1947 – remained in Britain. After her WAAF commission ended in mid-1945 Granville was faced with few prospects. Memos contained in her personnel file indicate that the British government didn't know quite what to do with her. Obviously there was no longer a need for her to work as a secret agent. Her lack of British citizenship meant she could not be considered for embassy work, and she had no clerical skills (nor interest in that type of work) to speak of. She received her divorce from Jerzy Giżycki in 1946, and over the next several years she took a number of menial jobs, such as a switchboard operator, waitress and shop assistant. She travelled frequently to Germany to see Kennedy, but was often restless and unhappy, constantly seeking the adrenalin rush that she missed so desperately. Vera Atkins stated bluntly, 'She was quite unable to adapt to boring day-to-day routine ... she lived for action and adventure.'[7]

In late 1950 Granville secured a position as a stewardess aboard the cruise ship *Rauhine*. She arrived in Glasgow on 1 May 1951 to join the ship for its maiden voyage. When it docked in London before setting sail for New Zealand, Kennedy flew in from Germany to see her off, and she told him how unhappy she was aboard the ship. The crew was not particularly friendly, and seemed to resent both her wartime decorations (which the crew were expected to wear) and her Polish nationality. As the ship set sail for its four-month voyage, Granville's unhappiness deepened. The work environment was uncomfortable, as she was alienated from most of the crew, but she did manage to make one friend, a steward named Dennis Muldowney. He was sympathetic to Granville's emotional state, and often helped her with her duties on the ship. They spent most of their free time together, and Muldowney claimed they became lovers.

When the ship returned to London in September 1951, Granville made a real effort to repay Muldowney's kindness by including him in her social circle. Her friends, including Kennedy, who had come to London to spend time with Granville, were puzzled by her attachment to Muldowney. One friend even said bluntly, 'It was obvious that he had a frightful inferiority complex. We used to wonder why he was with her. He did not come from her milieu, and he was definitely not her type. Christine always had a wide choice of stunning men, so why did she waste her time on a goblin like Muldowney?'[8]

As it had with so many other people, Granville's charm and beauty captivated Muldowney. He developed an obsessive interest in her, which eventually became too much for her to bear, and by November 1951 she was making a conscious effort to sever the relationship. She made social plans that did not include him, accepted a position on a ship that sailed to Australia without him and even told him to his face that he needed to leave her alone. Muldowney struggled with Granville's waning interest in him, and over the next several months his obsession with her grew. He stalked her at every opportunity and Granville grew increasingly frustrated with his behaviour. Muldowney erupted violently towards her one evening, and annoyed, rather than afraid, Granville instructed Muldowney in no uncertain terms to leave her alone. Completely fed up and seeking respite from her Muldowney drama, Granville made plans in June 1952 to leave London to escape his attentions. She arranged to reunite with Andrew Kennedy in Belgium, but before she could leave the country Muldowney struck. On 15 June 1952 Granville returned home to the hotel where she had been living. Muldowney was waiting for her. The two argued on the stairs and Granville once more told him to leave her alone. Enraged, Muldowney pinned her up against the wall and plunged a knife into her chest. Christine Granville, aged forty-four, died almost instantly.

Andrew Kennedy was immediately contacted, as he was listed as Granville's next of kin. He flew to London that same day, and took charge of arranging Granville's funeral. It was held on 20 June 1952, and was widely attended by her friends and colleagues. Christine Granville was buried at St Mary's Roman Catholic cemetery in north-west London. Dennis Muldowney made a full confession, and was hanged for his crime on 30 September 1952. Andrew Kennedy, who never married, returned to Germany, where he lived for the rest of his life. He died of cancer in December 1988, at the age of seventy-eight, and in accordance with his final wishes his ashes were taken to London and interred at the foot of Granville's grave.

Notes

Chapter 1: Violette Szabo

1. Ottaway, S., *Violette Szabo 'The Life That I Have…'* (London, 2002), p. 18.
2. The National Archive: SOE personnel files: Violette Szabo, ref.: HS9/1435.
3. Wake, N., *The White Mouse* (Melbourne, 1985), p. 111.
4. Perrin, N., *Spirit of Resistance* (Barnsley, 2008), p. 69.
5. The National Archive: SOE personnel files: Violette Szabo, ref.: HS9/1435.
6. Imperial War Museum, oral history interview with Oliver Brown, 1992.
7. Perrin, N., *Spirit of Resistance* (Barnsley, 2008), p. 115.
8. The National Archive: SOE personnel files: Violette Szabo, ref.: HS9/1435.
9. Ottaway, S., *Violette Szabo 'The Life That I Have'* (London, 2002), p. 108.
10. Perrin, N., *Spirit of Resistance* (Barnsley, 2008), p. 138.
11. *Ibid.*, p. 138.
12. *Ibid.*, p. 139.
13. Ottaway, S., *Violette Szabo 'The Life That I Have…'* (London, 2002), p. 146.
14. Imperial War Museum, oral history interview with Oliver Brown, 1992.

Chapter 2: Nancy Wake

1. Fitzsimons, P., *Nancy Wake* (Sydney, 2001), p. 49.
2. Wake, N., *The White Mouse* (Melbourne, 1985), p. 4.
3. *Ibid.*, p. 71.
4. Fitzsimons, P., *Nancy Wake* (Sydney, 2001), p. 173.
5. Wake, N., *The White Mouse* (Melbourne, 1985), p. 104.
6. Fitzsimons, P., *Nancy Wake* (Sydney, 2001), p. 176.
7. Wake, N., *The White Mouse* (Melbourne, 1985), p. 106.
8. *Ibid.*, p. 121.
9. Roper, M., 'The White Mouse: Girl Who Gave the Nazis Hell' in *The Mirror* (London, 9 August 2011), p. 24.
10. Wake, N., *The White Mouse* (Melbourne, 1985), p. 135.
11. *Ibid.*, p. 148.
12. Roper, M., 'The White Mouse: Girl Who Gave the Nazis Hell' in *The Mirror* (London, 9 August 2011), p. 24.
13. Brace, M., 'Heroine Australia Snubbed Moves to Britain' in *The Evening Standard* (London, 10 December 2001), p. 19.
14. Fitzsimons, P., *Nancy Wake* (Sydney, 2001), p. 297.

Chapter 3: Noor Inayat Khan

1. Fuller, Jean Overton, *Noor-un-nisa Inayat Khan* (London, 1971), p. 84.
2. The National Archive: SOE personnel files: Noor Inayat Khan, ref.: HS9/836/5.
3. *Ibid.*
4. *Ibid.*
5. Basu, Shrabani, *Spy Princess: The Life of Noor Inayat Khan* (New York, 2007),
   p. 78.
6. *Ibid.*, p. 85.
7. *Ibid.*, p. 89.
8. The National Archive: SOE personnel files: Noor Inayat Khan, ref.: HS9/836/5.

9. The National Archive: SOE personnel files: Noor Inayat Khan, ref.: HS9/836/5.

10. Buckmaster, Maurice, *Specially Employed* (London, 1952), p. 31.

11. The National Archive: SOE personnel files: Noor Inayat Khan, ref.: HS9/836/5.

12. Fuller, Jean Overton, *Noor-un-nisa Inayat Khan* (London, 1971), p. 139.

13. The National Archive: SOE personnel files: Noor Inayat Khan, ref.: HS9/836/5.

14. *Ibid.*

15. *Ibid.*

16. *Ibid.*

17. Fuller, Jean Overton, *Noor-un-nisa Inayat Khan* (London, 1971), p. 208.

18. The National Archive: SOE personnel files: Noor Inayat Khan, ref.: HS9/836/5.

19. *Ibid.*

20. *Ibid.*

21. Basu, Shrabani, *Spy Princess: The Life of Noor Inayat Khan* (New York, 2007), p. 175.

22. Fuller, Jean Overton, *Noor-un-nisa Inayat Khan* (London, 1971), p. 253.

23. Basu, Shrabani, *Spy Princess: The Life of Noor Inayat Khan* (New York, 2007), p. 175.

Chapter 4: Sonia Butt

1. 'She Ate With Gestapo – Killed Some? Why, Sure' in *Toronto Star* (2 December 1945), p. 3.

2. Stafford, D., *Ten Days to D-Day* (New York, 2003), p. 107.

3. d'Artois, Sonia (as told to Ann Frommer), 'I Was A Woman Spy' in *Coronet Magazine* (May 1954), p. 162.

4. *Ibid.*, p. 163.

5. *Ibid.*, p. 163.

6. *Ibid.*, p. 164.
7. Hudson, S., *Undercover Operator* (Barnsley, 2003), p. 67.
8. Champkin, Julian, 'The Designer Spy' in *The Daily Mail* (1 May 2004).
9. d'Artois, Sonia (as told to Ann Frommer), 'I Was A Woman Spy' in *Coronet Magazine* (May 1954), p. 165.
10. *Ibid.*, p. 167.
11. *Ibid.*, p. 167.
12. 'Sonia Was a Spy' in *Maclean's Magazine* (15 February 1953), p. 46.
13. d'Artois, Sonia (as told to Ann Frommer), 'I Was A Woman Spy' in *Coronet Magazine* (May 1954), p. 162.
14. *Ibid.*, p. 165.
15. 'Sonia Was a Spy' in *Maclean's Magazine* (15 February 1953), p. 47.
16. *Ibid.*, p. 46.
17. Hudson, S., *Undercover Operator* (Barnsley, 2003), p. 105.
18. Interview with Nadya d'Artois Murdoch, 9 August 2013.
19. *Ibid.*
20 Branswell, Brenda, 'Obituary: Former Hudson resident Sonia D'Artois served as undercover British Agent', *The Montreal Gazette* (2 January 2015).
21. 'The White Mouse That Roared' in *The Sunshine Coast Daily* (13 August 2011).
22. Branswell, Brenda, 'Obituary: Former Hudson resident Sonia D'Artois served as undercover British Agent', *The Montreal Gazette* (2 January 2015).

Chapter 5: Diana Rowden

1. The National Archive: SOE personnel files: Diana Rowden, ref.: HS9/1287/6.
2. *Ibid.*
3. Author interview with Robert Maloubier, Paris, 2005.
4. Nicholas, E., *Death Be Not Proud* (London, 1958), p. 36.

5. *Ibid.*, p. 140.
6. *Ibid.*, p. 156.
7. Churchill, P., *The Spirit in the Cage* (New York, 1955), p. 103.
8. Kramer, R., *Flames in the Field* (London, 1995), p. 119.
9. *Ibid.*, p. 121.
10. Nicholas, E., *Death Be Not Proud* (London, 1958), p. 61.
11. *Ibid.*, p. 61.
12. *Ibid.*, p. 61.
13. *Ibid.*, p. 34.

Chapter 6: Odette Sansom

1. Imperial War Museum, oral history interview with Odette Hallowes, 1985.
2. Starns, P., *Odette: World War Two's Darling Spy* (Stroud, 2009), p. 19.
3. The National Archive: SOE personnel files: Odette Sansom, ref.: HS9/648/4.
4. Imperial War Museum, oral history interview with Odette Hallowes, 1985.
5. The National Archive: SOE personnel files: Odette Sansom, ref.: HS9/648/4.
6. Imperial War Museum, oral history interview with Oliver Brown, 1992.
7. Imperial War Museum, oral history interview with Odette Hallowes, 1985.
8. Imperial War Museum, oral history interview with Odette Hallowes, 1985.
9. Imperial War Museum, oral history interview with Odette Hallowes, 1985.
10. The National Archive: SOE personnel files: Odette Sansom, ref.: HS9/648/4.
11. The National Archive: SOE personnel files: Odette Sansom, ref.: HS9/648/4.

12. Imperial War Museum, oral history interview with Odette Hallowes, 1985.
13. *The Sunday Herald* (Sydney, NSW), 7 October 1951. http://trove.nla.gov.au/ndp/del/article/18491083

Chapter 7: Mathilde Carré

1. Carré, M., *I Was 'The Cat'* (London, 1960), p. 16.
2. *Ibid.*, p. 16.
3. *Ibid.*, p. 17.
4. *Ibid.*, p. 79.
5. *Ibid.*, p. 86.
6. Young, G., *The Cat with Two Faces* (New York, 1957), p. 222.
7. Carré, M., *I Was 'The Cat'* (London, 1960), p. 115.
8. The National Archive: Mathilde Lucie Carré, alias Victoire, La Chatte, ref.: KV 2/927.
9. *Ibid.*
10. Young, G., *The Cat with Two Faces* (New York, 1957), p. 179.

Chapter 8: Christine Granville

1. Mulley, C., *The Spy Who Loved* (New York, 2012), p. 22.
2. *Ibid.*, p. 25.
3. The National Archive: SOE personnel files: Christine Granville, ref.: HS9/612.
4. Imperial War Museum, oral history interview with Brooks Richards, 1987.
5. Mulley, C., *The Spy Who Loved* (New York, 2012), p. 204.
6. The National Archive: SOE personnel files: Christine Granville, ref.: HS9/612.
7. Mulley, C., *The Spy Who Loved* (New York, 2012), p. 331.
8. *Ibid.*, p. 320.

Bibliography

Atwood, Kathryn, *Women Heroes of World War II* (Chicago: 2011)

Basu, Shrabani, *Spy Princess: The Life of Noor Inayat Khan* (New York: 2007)

Binney, Marcus, *The Women Who Lived For Danger* (New York: 2002)

Brace, M., 'Heroine Australia Snubbed Moves to Britain' in *The Evening Standard* (London: 10 December 2001)

Braddon, Russell, *Nancy Wake* (London: 1956)

Branswell, Brenda, 'Obituary: Former Hudson resident Sonia D'Artois served as undercover British Agent', *The Montreal Gazette* (2 January 2015)

Buckmaster, Maurice, *Specially Employed: The Story of British Aid to French Patriots of the Resistance* (London: 1958)

Carré, Mathilde, *I Was 'The Cat'* (London: 1960)

Champkin, Julian, 'The Designer Spy' in *The Daily Mail* (1 May 2004)

Churchill, Peter, *Duel of Wits* (London: 1953)

Churchill, Peter, *The Spirit in the Cage* (New York: 1955)

Cookridge, E. H., *They Came from the Sky* (London: 1966)

Cunningham, Cyril, *Beaulieu: The Finishing School for Secret Agents* (London: 1998)

d'Artois, Sonia (as told to Anne Frommer), 'I Was a Woman Spy' in *Coronet Magazine* (May 1954)

Fitzsimons, Peter, *Nancy Wake* (Sydney: 2001)

Foot, M. R. D., *SOE in France: An Account of the Work of the British Special Operations*

Executive in France 1940–1944 (London: 2004)

Fuller, Jean Overton, *Madeleine: The Story of Noor Inayat Khan* (London: 1952)

Fuller, Jean Overton, *The German Penetration of SOE* (London: 1975)

Helm, Sarah, *A Life in Secrets: The Story of Vera Atkins and the Lost Agents of SOE* (London: 2005)

Howarth, Patrick, *Undercover: The Men and Women of the SOE* (London: 2000)

Hudson, Sydney, *Undercover Operator: An SOE Agent's Experiences in France and the Far East* (Barnsley: 2003)

Kramer, Rita, *Flames in the Field* (London: 1995)

MacLaren, Roy, *Canadians Behind Enemy Lines 1939–1945* (Vancouver: 1981)

Marks, Leo, *Between Silk and Cyanide* (London: 1998)

Marshall, Bruce, *The White Rabbit* (London: 1952)

Masson, Madeleine, *Christine: A Search for Christine Granville* (London: 1975)

Miller, Russell, *Behind the Lines: The Oral History of Special Operations in World War II* (New York: 2002)

Minney, R. J., *Carve Her Name with Pride* (London: 1956)

Mulley, Clare, *The Spy Who Loved: The Secrets and Lives of Christine Granville* (New York: 2012)

Nicholas, Elizabeth, *Death Be Not Proud* (London: 1958)

Ottaway, Susan, *Sisters, Secrets and Sacrifice* (London: 2013)

Ottaway, Susan, *Violette Szabo 'The Life That I Have...'* (London: 2002)

Paine, Lauran, *Mathilde Carré: Double Agent* (London: 1976)

Perrin, Nigel, *The Spirit of Resistance* (Barnsley: 2008)

Polmar, Norman and Thomas Allen, *Spy Book: The Encyclopedia of Espionage* (New York: 1998)

Porter, Mackenzie, 'Sonia Was a Spy' in *MacLean's Magazine* (15 February 1953)

Roper, M., 'The White Mouse: Girl Who Gave the Nazis Hell' in *The Mirror* (London, 9 August 2011)

'She Ate With Gestapo-Killed Some? Why, Sure' in *The Toronto Star* (2 December 1945)

Stafford, David, *Ten Days to D-Day* (New York: 2001)

Starns, Penny, *Odette: World War Two's Darling Spy* (Stroud: 2009)

Stevenson, William, *A Man Called Intrepid* (New York: 1976)

'The White Mouse That Roared' in *The Sunshine Coast Daily* (13 August 2011)

Tickell, Jerrad, *Odette* (London: 1949)

Wake, Nancy, *The White Mouse* (Melbourne: 1985)

Wynne, Barry, *No Drums ... No Trumpets: The Story of Mary Lindell* (London: 1961)

Websites

http://www.bbc.co.uk/history/worldwars/wwtwo/soe_01.shtml

http://www.bbc.co.uk/history/worldwars/wwtwo/soe_training_01.shtm

http://www.our-secret-war.org/Introduction.html

http://soe_french.tripod.com/

http://trove.nla.gov.au/ndp/del/article/18491083

Interviews

Martyn Cox, oral historian (July 2013)

Nadya Murdoch, daughter of Sonia Butt d'Artois (August 2013)

Robert Maloubier, SOE agent, colleague and friend of Violette Szabo and Diana Rowden (August 2005)

Public Archives

The National Archives, Kew:

HS 9/183   Personnel file of Christine Granville

HS 9/648/4   Personnel file of Odette Sansom

HS 9/836/5   Personnel file of Noor Inayat Khan
HS 9/1287/6   Personnel file of Diana Rowden
HS 9/1435   Personnel file of Violette Szabo
KV 2/927   Mathilde Lucie Carré, alias Victoire, La Chatte

The Imperial War Museum, London Sound Archive:
4843, George Abbott
9331, Selwyn Jepsom
9452, Maurice Buckmaster
9478, Odette Sansom Hallowes
9551, Vera Atkins
9697, Robin Brook
9827, Patrick Howarth
9970, Sir Francis Brooks Richards
11087, Gwendolyn Lees
12423, Oliver Brown

About the Author

Robyn Walker is a teacher-librarian and historian. She has ten years of publishing experience in books, magazines and journals. This is her second book dealing with aspects of the Second World War. Her first book was shortlisted for an award at the Children's Literature Roundtable Information Book Award. She lives in St Thomas, Ontario.

Index

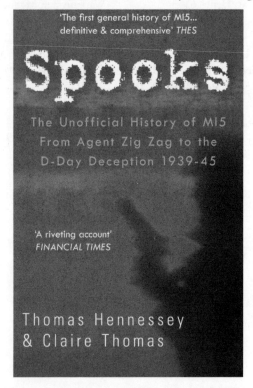

Also available from Amberley Publishing

FRANK MEERES

SUFFRAGETTES

How Britain's women fought
& died for the right to vote

'A fascinating overview of the
women's suffrage movement'
BBC WHO DO YOU THINK YOU ARE?

Available from all good bookshops or to order direct
Please call **01453-847-800**
www.amberleybooks.com